AT THE MOUNTAINS OF MADNESS

A GRAPHIC NOVEL

AT THE MOUNTAINS OF MADNESS

A GRAPHIC NOVEL

ADAPTED FROM THE ORIGINAL NOVEL BY
H.P. LOVECRAFT
TEXT ADAPTED AND ILLUSTRATED BY
I.N.J. CULBARD

SELF
MADE
HERO

First published 2010
by SelfMadeHero
A division of Metro Media Ltd
5 Upper Wimpole Street
London W1G 6BP
www.selfmadehero.com

Illustrator and Adaptor: I.N.J. Culbard
Cover Designer: I.N.J. Culbard
Layout Designer: Andy Huckle
Textual Consultant: Nick de Somogyi
Publishing Director: Emma Hayley
Marketing Director: Doug Wallace
With thanks to: Dan Lockwood

Dedication
For Katy, Joseph and Benjamin
— I. N. J. Culbard

A CIP record for this book is available from the British Library

ISBN: 978-1-906838-12-6

10 9 8 7 6 5 4 3 2 1

Printed and bound in China

FOREWORD

Written in 1931, *At the Mountains of Madness* is a key work in H.P. Lovecraft's canon. Originally rejected by *Weird Tales*, the novel has since become a firm favourite with readers of the macabre. A haunting combination of science and fantasy in its own right, the novel also explains and connects various elements of Lovecraft's "Cthulhu mythos". Indeed, these pages – with their references to Miskatonic University, the dreaded *Necronomicon* and a host of monstrous beings – contain much that will be familiar to devoted Lovecraft fans. For those who have yet to venture into the unknown, *At the Mountains of Madness* is both accessible and exciting, and stands as one of Lovecraft's most successful tales.

Antarctica – then, as now, one of the least explored areas of the world – marks something of a departure for Lovecraft in terms of setting. As soon as his characters arrived on that mysterious continent, Lovecraft's imagination ran unchecked – he was able to fill the landscape with impossible, malevolent cities, safe in the knowledge that he was unlikely to be contradicted by scientific fact (for a while, at least). This freedom allowed for a sense of scale which is unmatched in Lovecraft's other works. The vast polar wasteland is swiftly established as an enthralling, terrifying location, producing a creeping atmosphere of horror before we have even been introduced to its inhabitants.

Infirm for much of his life, Lovecraft's intolerance (bordering on horror) of cold temperatures is reflected in the pervading sense of doom which runs through his tale. However, this abhorrence is somewhat countered by Lovecraft's fascination with polar exploration. As a result, *At the Mountains of Madness* is a compelling mixture of the repellent and the intriguing; the friction between these two states makes this one of Lovecraft's most powerful stories. Ian Culbard's sterling adaptation captures this antagonism perfectly, conjuring up the *Boy's Own* thrill of exploration before hitting us with a series of horrifying discoveries, each with greater implications for man's place in the universe.

"*At the Mountains of Madness* represents the most serious work I have attempted," Lovecraft wrote, "and its rejection was a very discouraging influence." Although he never found popular success during his lifetime, that dispiriting rejection has proved to be unfounded. This adaptation confirms the book's standing among the very best of genre fiction.

— Dan Lockwood
editor, *The Lovecraft Anthology: Vol I* (2011)

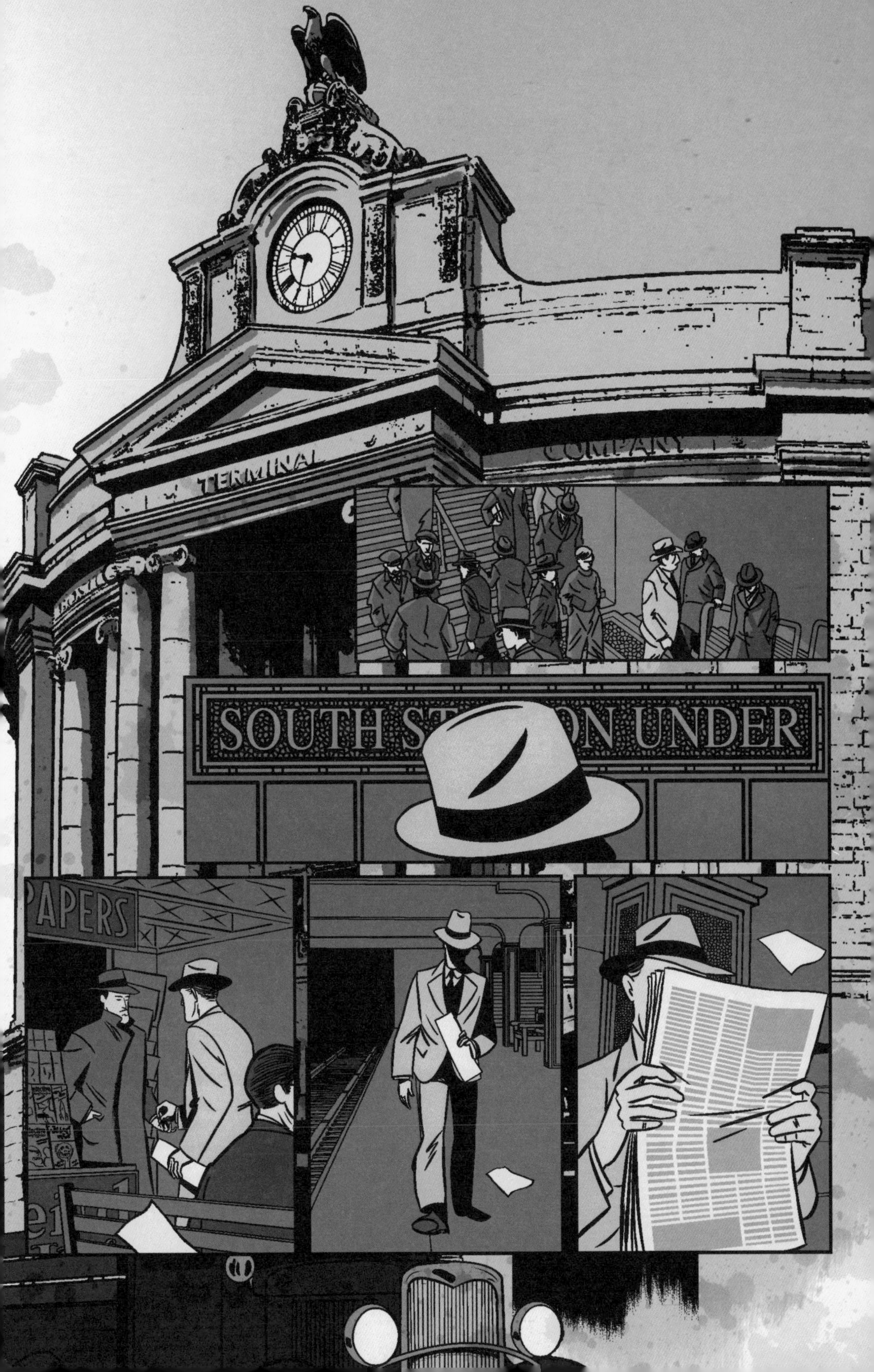
TERMINAL
COMPANY
SOUTH ST ON UNDER
PAPERS

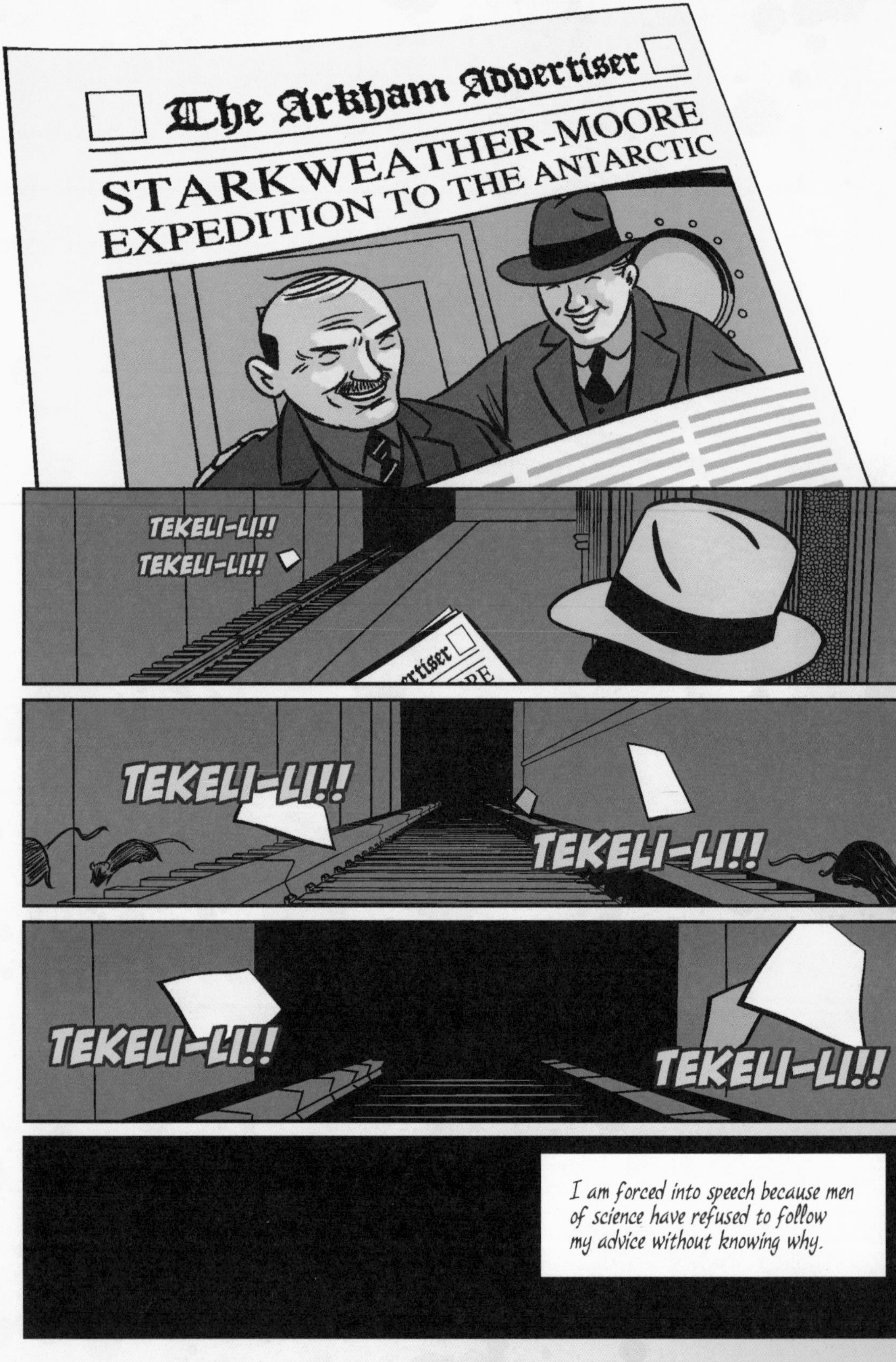
The Arkham Advertiser
STARKWEATHER-MOORE
EXPEDITION TO THE ANTARCTIC
TEKELI-LI!!
TEKELI-LI!!
TEKELI-LI!!
TEKELI-LI!!
TEKELI-LI!!
TEKELI-LI!!
I am forced into speech because men of science have refused to follow my advice without knowing why.

It is with considerable reluctance I disclose my reasons for opposing the **Starkweather-Moore** expedition to the Antarctic — the more so because my warning may be in vain.

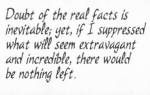

Doubt of the real facts is inevitable; yet, if I suppressed what will seem extravagant and incredible, there would be nothing left.

The photographs will be regarded as nothing more than clever fakes and my ink drawings will be jeered at as obvious impostures.

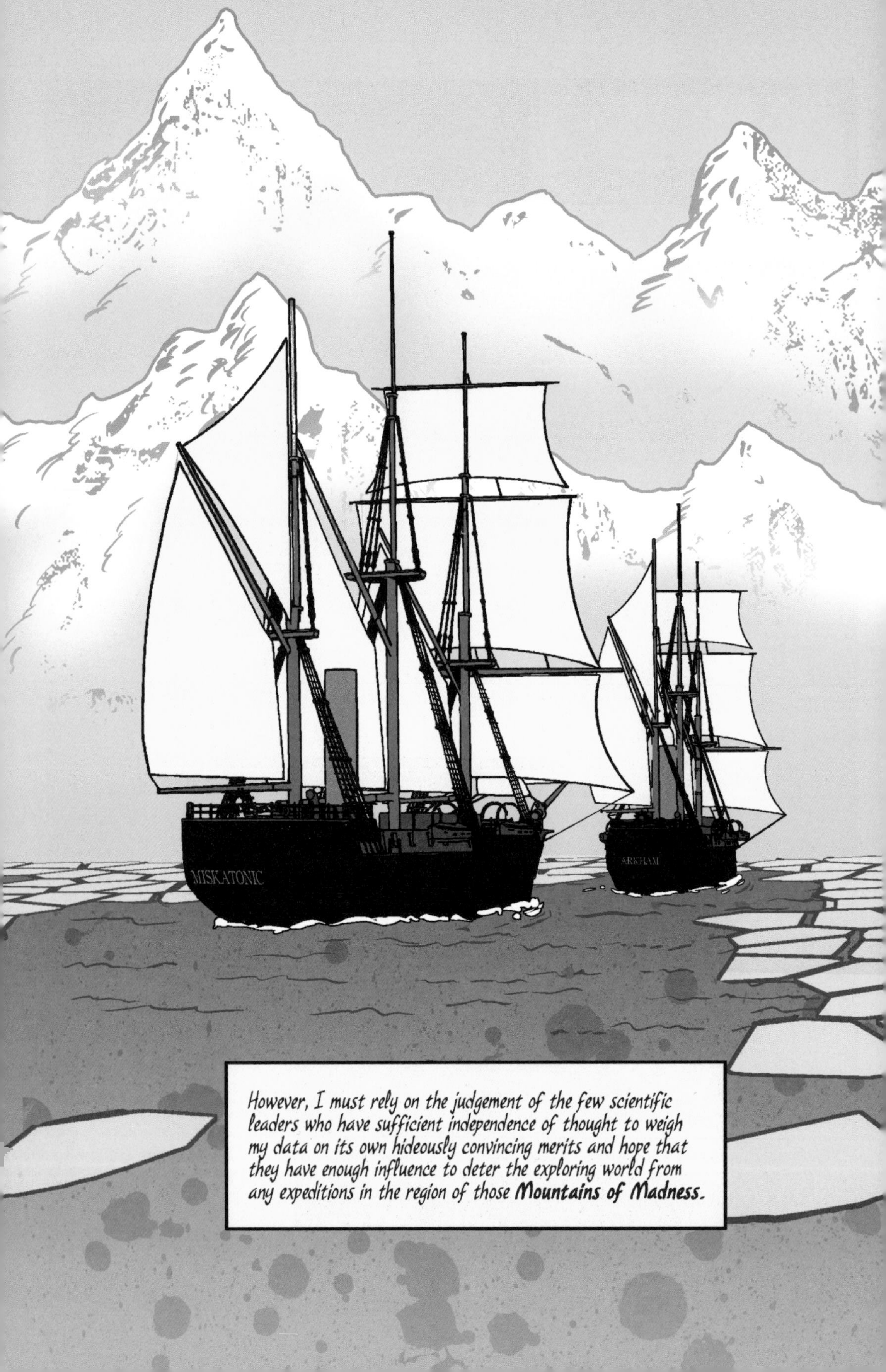
MISKATONIC
ARKHAM
However, I must rely on the judgement of the few scientific leaders who have sufficient independence of thought to weigh my data on its own hideously convincing merits and hope that they have enough influence to deter the exploring world from any expeditions in the region of those **Mountains of Madness**.

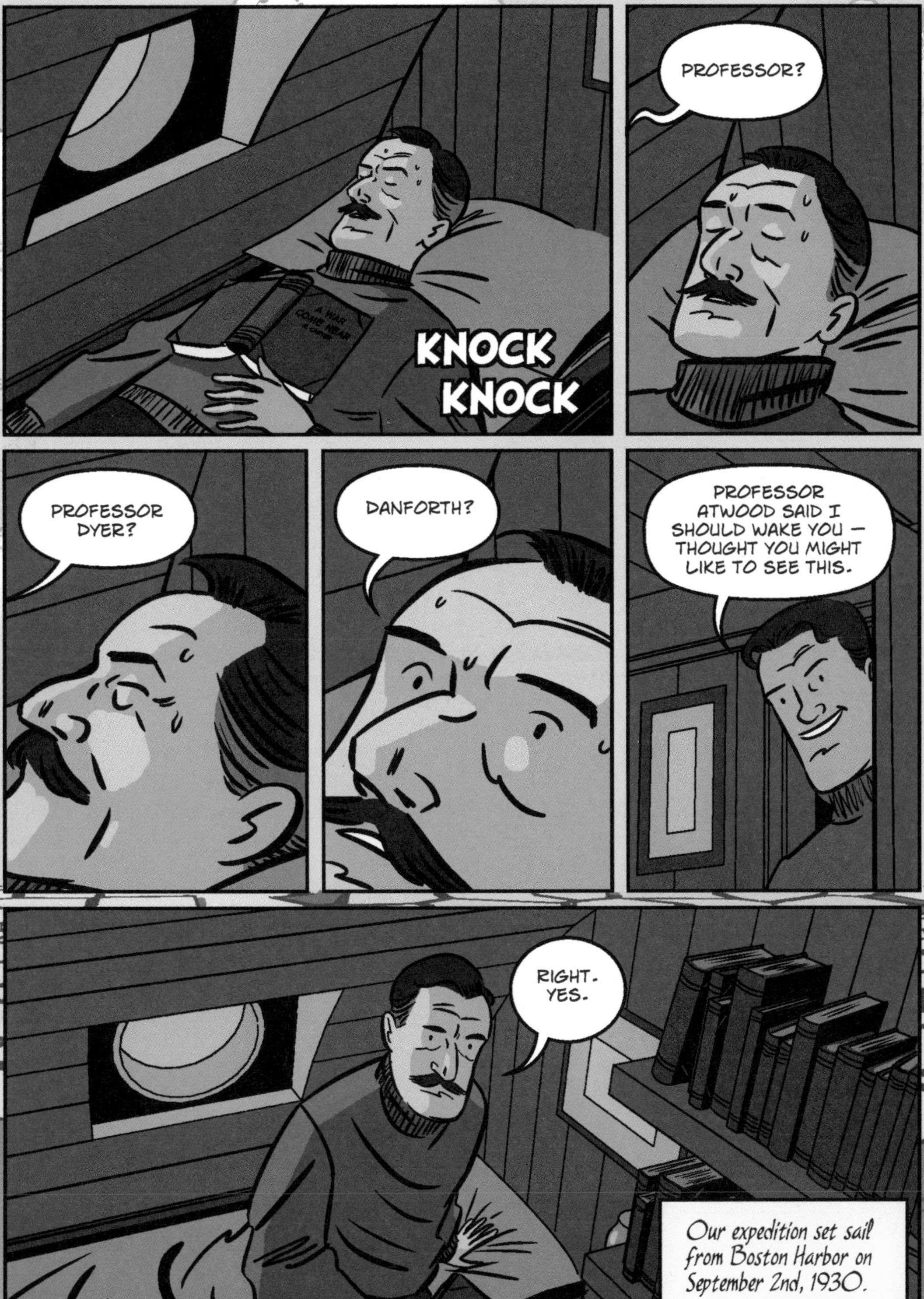
KNOCK
KNOCK
PROFESSOR?
PROFESSOR
DYER?
DANFORTH?
PROFESSOR
ATWOOD SAID I
SHOULD WAKE YOU —
THOUGHT YOU MIGHT
LIKE TO SEE THIS.
RIGHT.
YES.
Our expedition set sail
from Boston Harbor on
September 2nd, 1930.

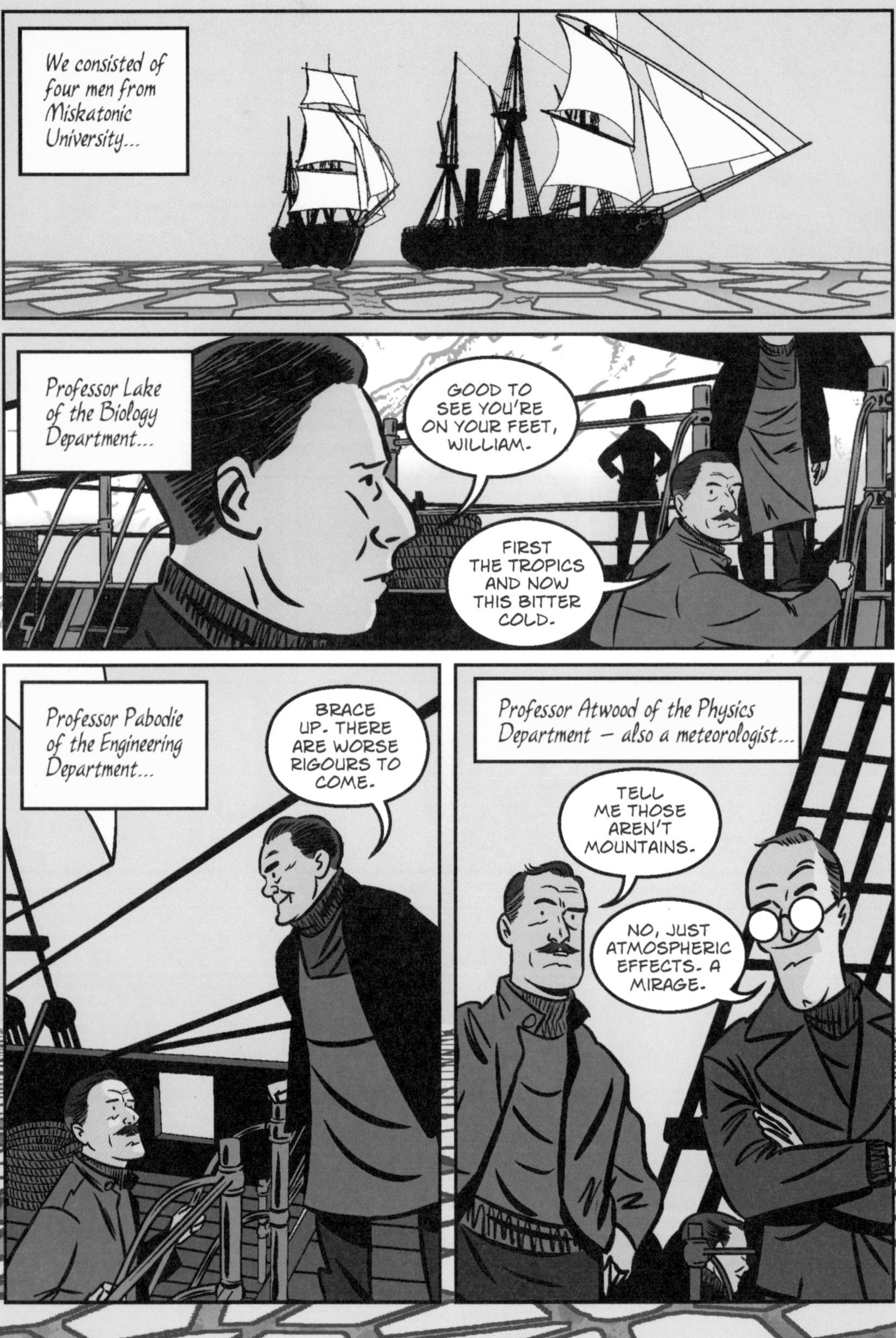

We consisted of four men from Miskatonic University...
Professor Lake of the Biology Department...
GOOD TO SEE YOU'RE ON YOUR FEET, WILLIAM.
FIRST THE TROPICS AND NOW THIS BITTER COLD.
Professor Pabodie of the Engineering Department...
BRACE UP. THERE ARE WORSE RIGOURS TO COME.
Professor Atwood of the Physics Department — also a meteorologist...
TELL ME THOSE AREN'T MOUNTAINS.
NO, JUST ATMOSPHERIC EFFECTS. A MIRAGE.

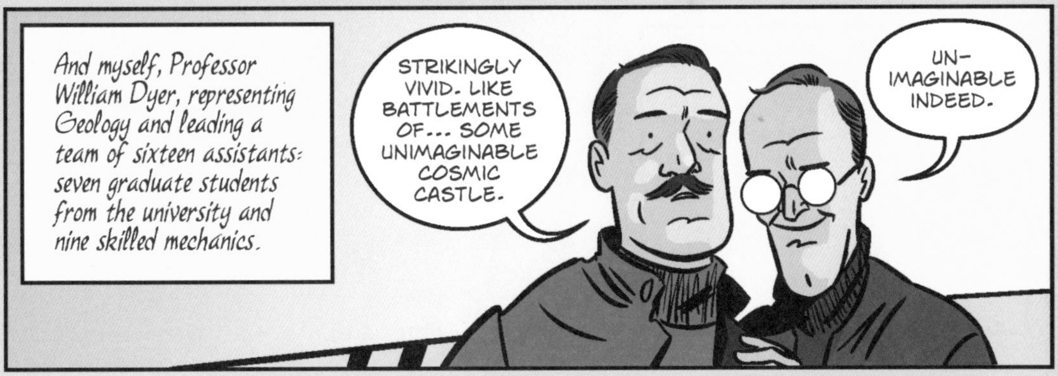
And myself, Professor William Dyer, representing Geology and leading a team of sixteen assistants: seven graduate students from the university and nine skilled mechanics.
STRIKINGLY VIVID. LIKE BATTLEMENTS OF... SOME UNIMAGINABLE COSMIC CASTLE.
UN-IMAGINABLE INDEED.

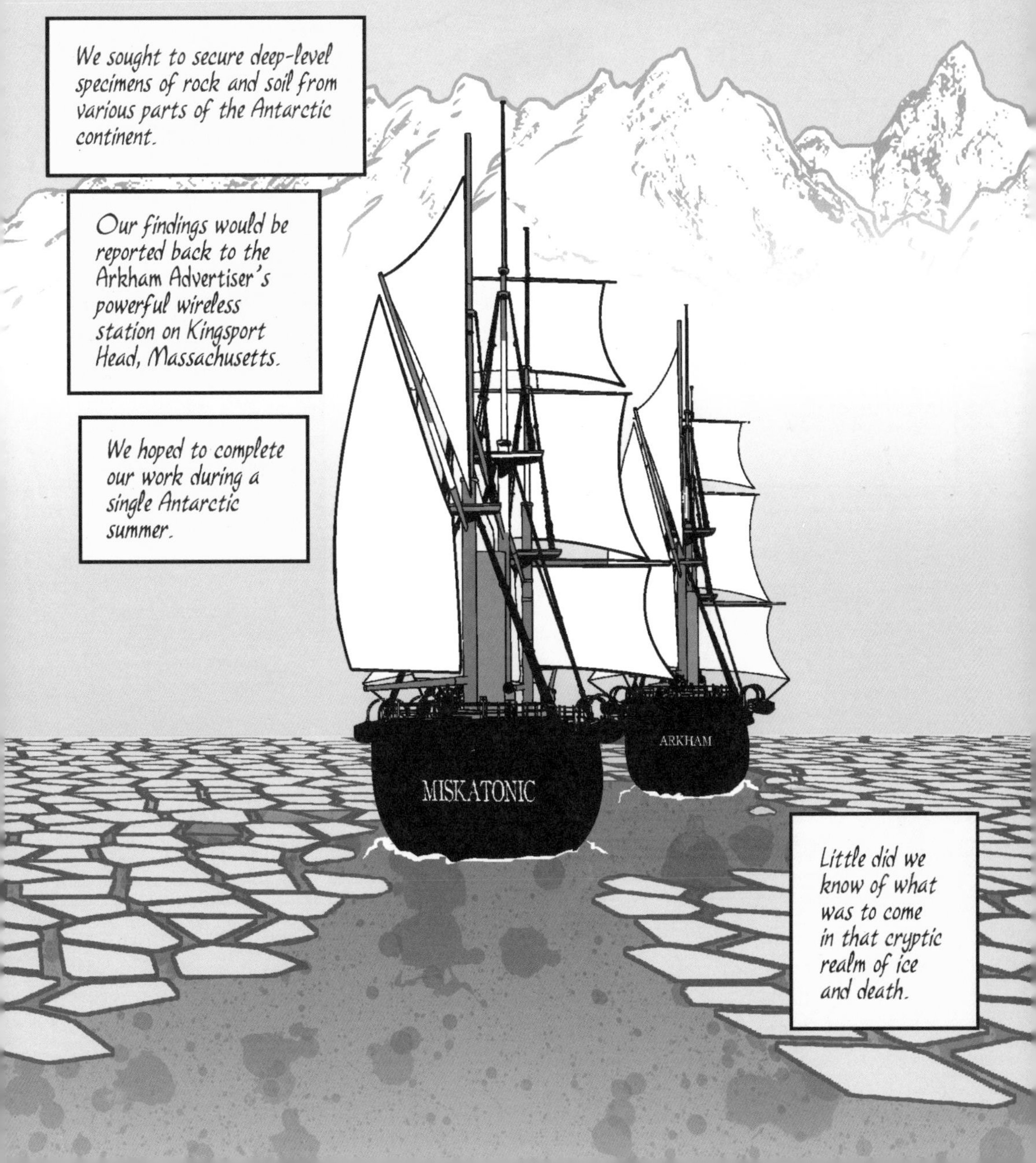
We sought to secure deep-level specimens of rock and soil from various parts of the Antarctic continent.
Our findings would be reported back to the Arkham Advertiser's powerful wireless station on Kingsport Head, Massachusetts.
We hoped to complete our work during a single Antarctic summer.
ARKHAM
MISKATONIC
Little did we know of what was to come in that cryptic realm of ice and death.

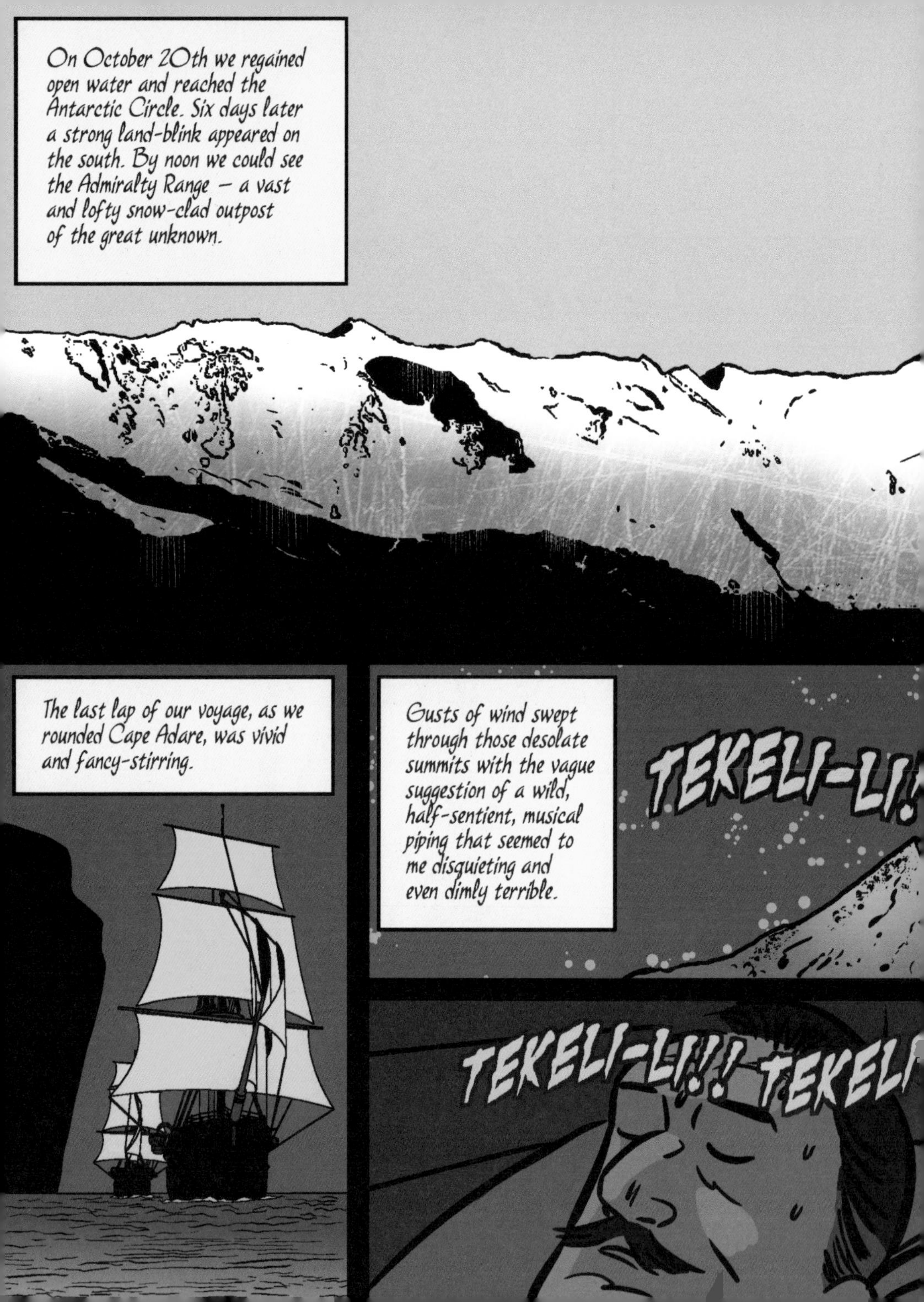
On October 20th we regained open water and reached the Antarctic Circle. Six days later a strong land-blink appeared on the south. By noon we could see the Admiralty Range – a vast and lofty snow-clad outpost of the great unknown.
The last lap of our voyage, as we rounded Cape Adare, was vivid and fancy-stirring.
Gusts of wind swept through those desolate summits with the vague suggestion of a wild, half-sentient, musical piping that seemed to me disquieting and even dimly terrible.
TEKELI-LI!
TEKELI-LI!! TEKELI

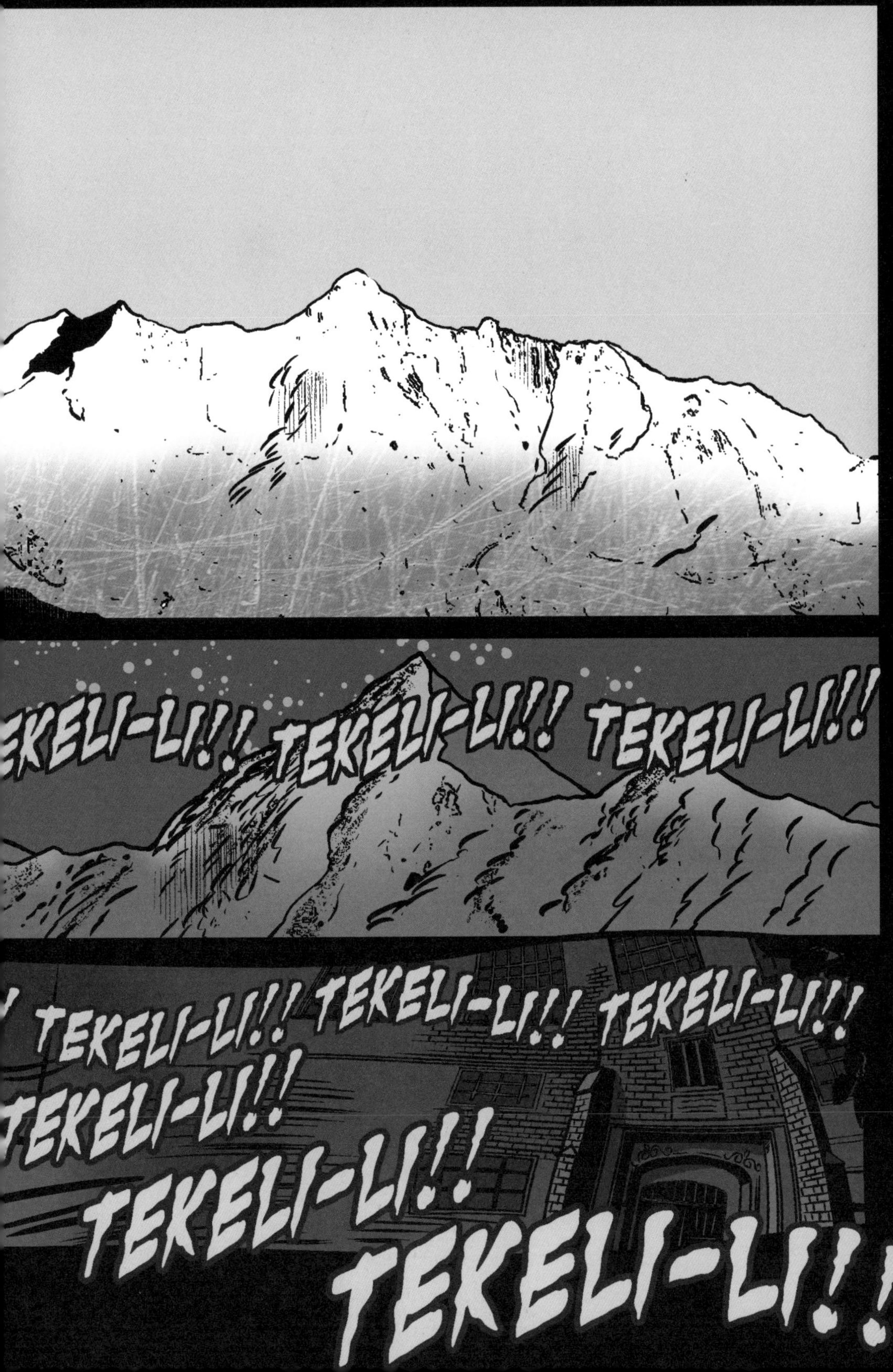
EKELI-LI!!
TEKELI-LI!!
TEKELI-LI!!
TEKELI-LI!!
TEKELI-LI!!
TEKELI-LI!!
EKELI-LI!!
TEKELI-LI!!
TEKELI-LI!!

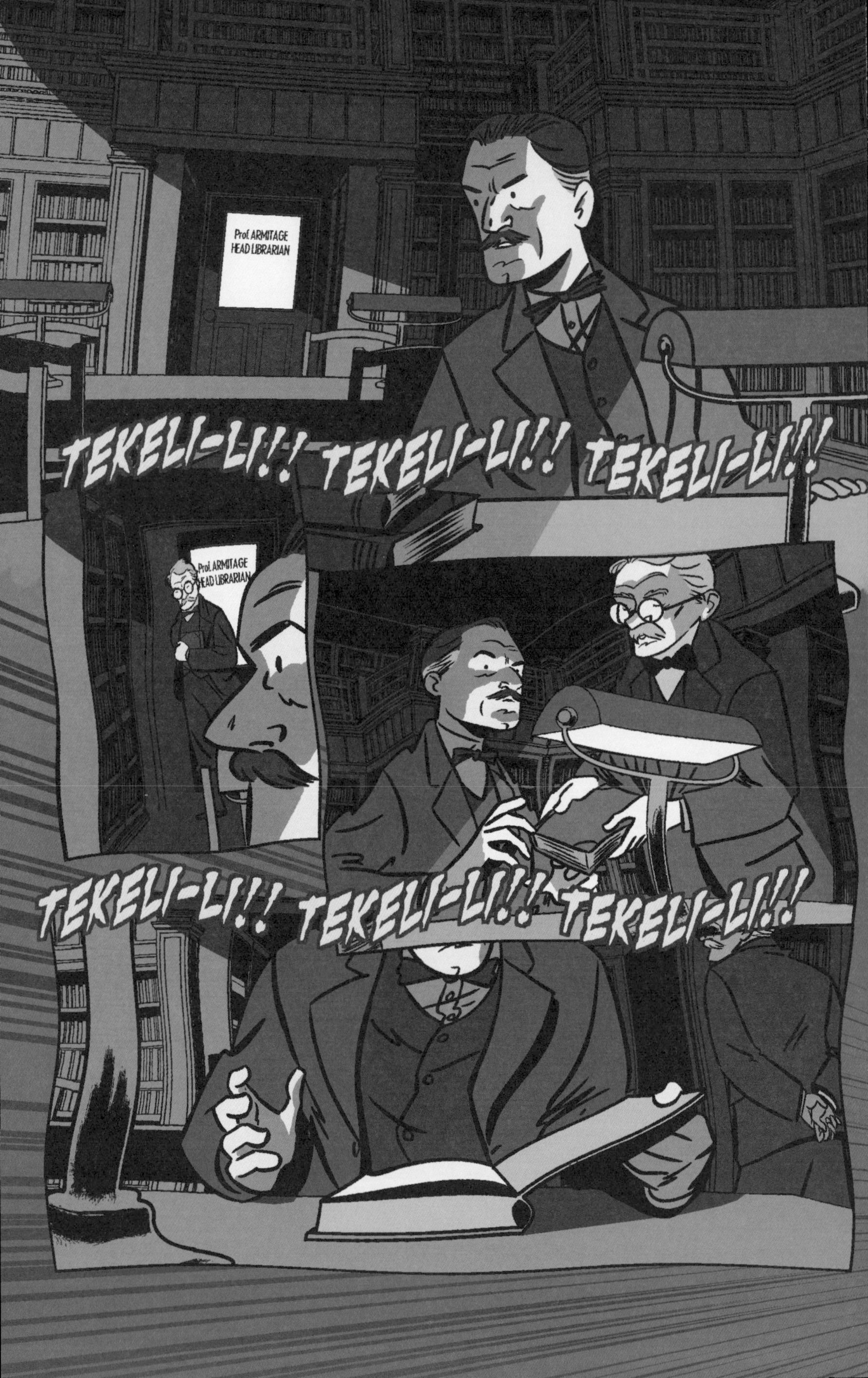
Prof. ARMITAGE
HEAD LIBRARIAN
TEKELI-LI!! TEKELI-LI!! TEKELI-LI!!
Prof. ARMITAGE
HEAD LIBRARIAN
TEKELI-LI!! TEKELI-LI!! TEKELI-LI!!

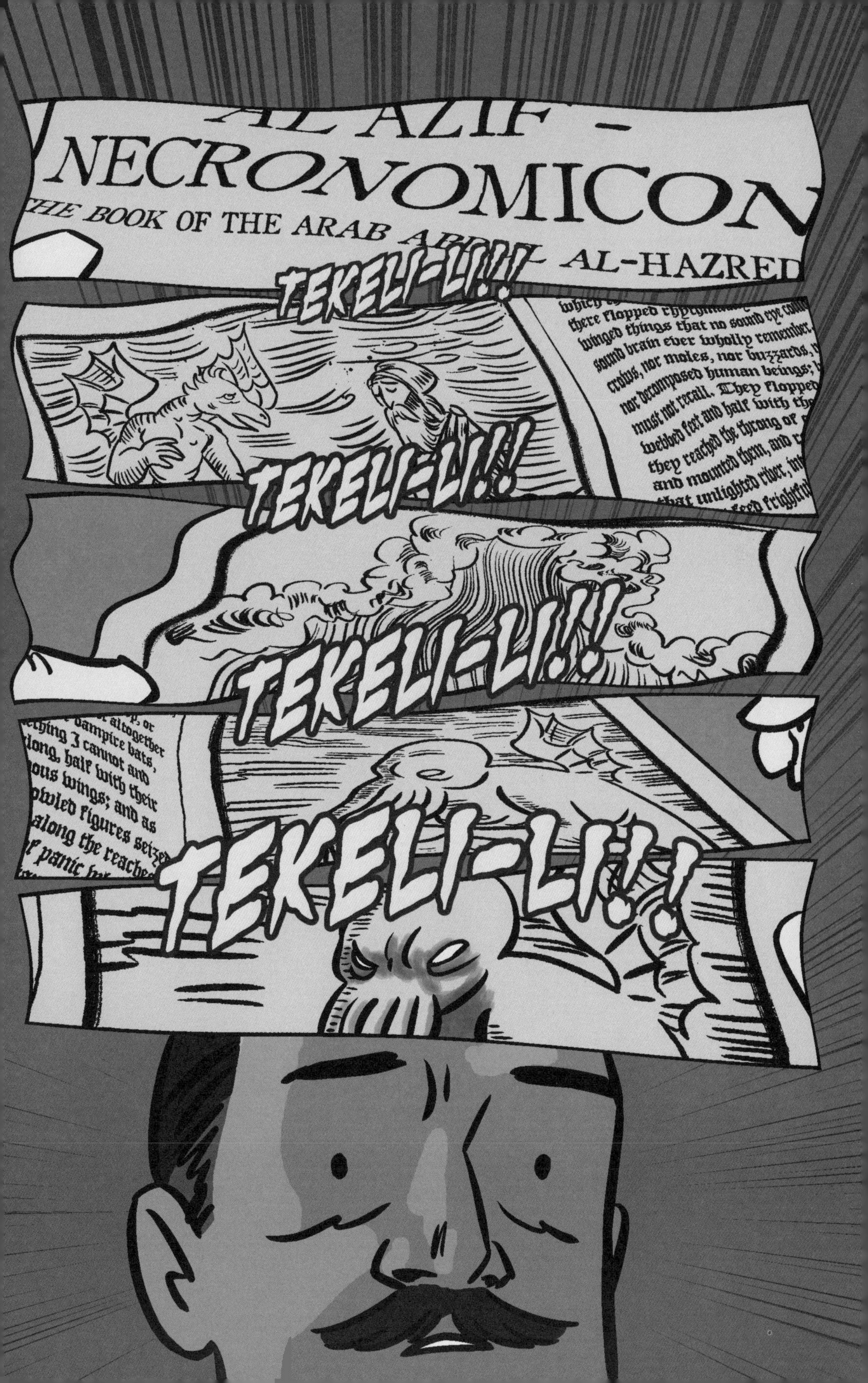
AL AZIF –
NECRONOMICON
TEKELI-LI!!
TEKELI-LI!!
TEKELI-LI!!
TEKELI-LI!!

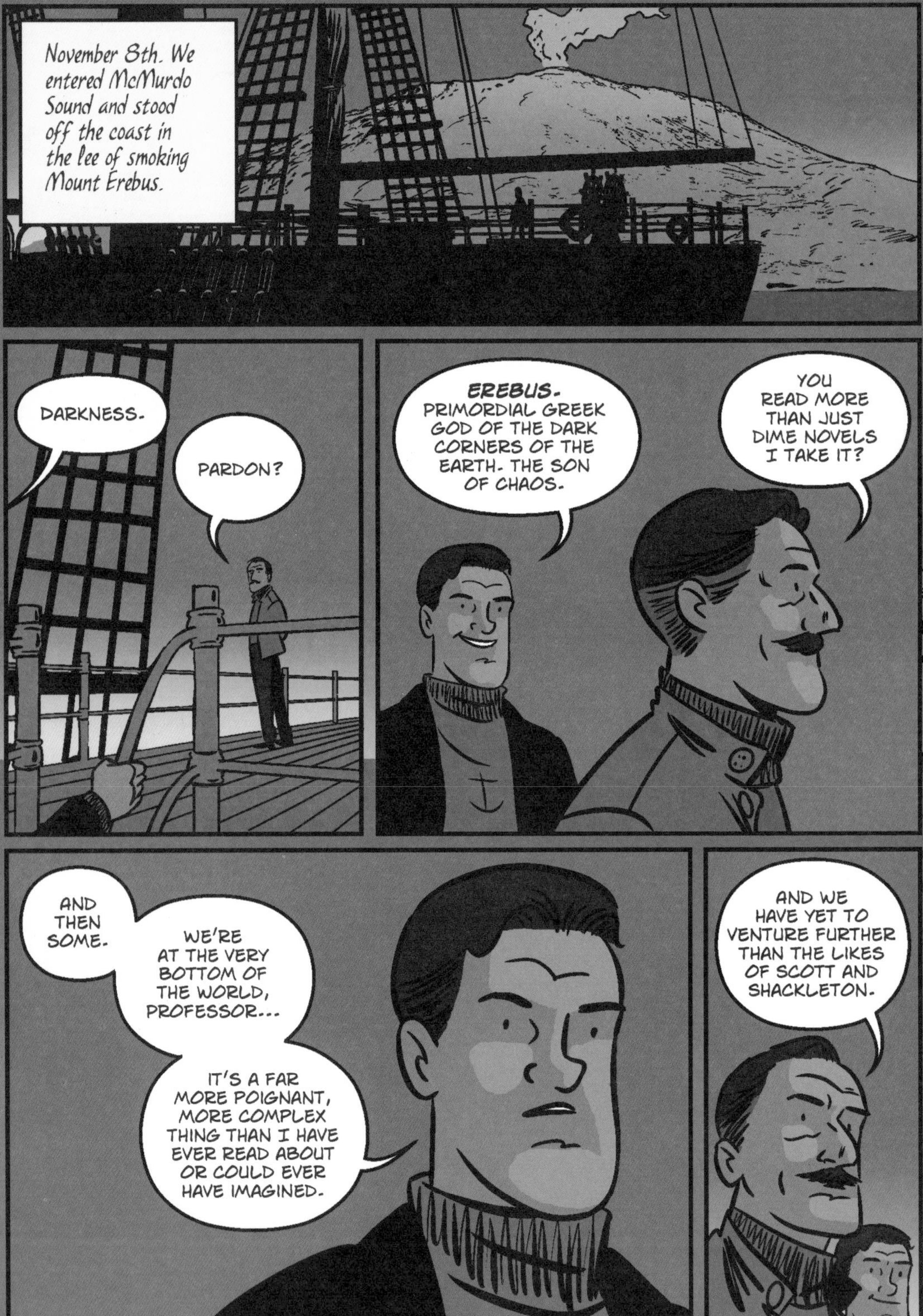
November 8th. We entered McMurdo Sound and stood off the coast in the lee of smoking Mount Erebus.
DARKNESS.
PARDON?
EREBUS. PRIMORDIAL GREEK GOD OF THE DARK CORNERS OF THE EARTH. THE SON OF CHAOS.
YOU READ MORE THAN JUST DIME NOVELS I TAKE IT?
AND THEN SOME.
WE'RE AT THE VERY BOTTOM OF THE WORLD, PROFESSOR...
IT'S A FAR MORE POIGNANT, MORE COMPLEX THING THAN I HAVE EVER READ ABOUT OR COULD EVER HAVE IMAGINED.
AND WE HAVE YET TO VENTURE FURTHER THAN THE LIKES OF SCOTT AND SHACKLETON.

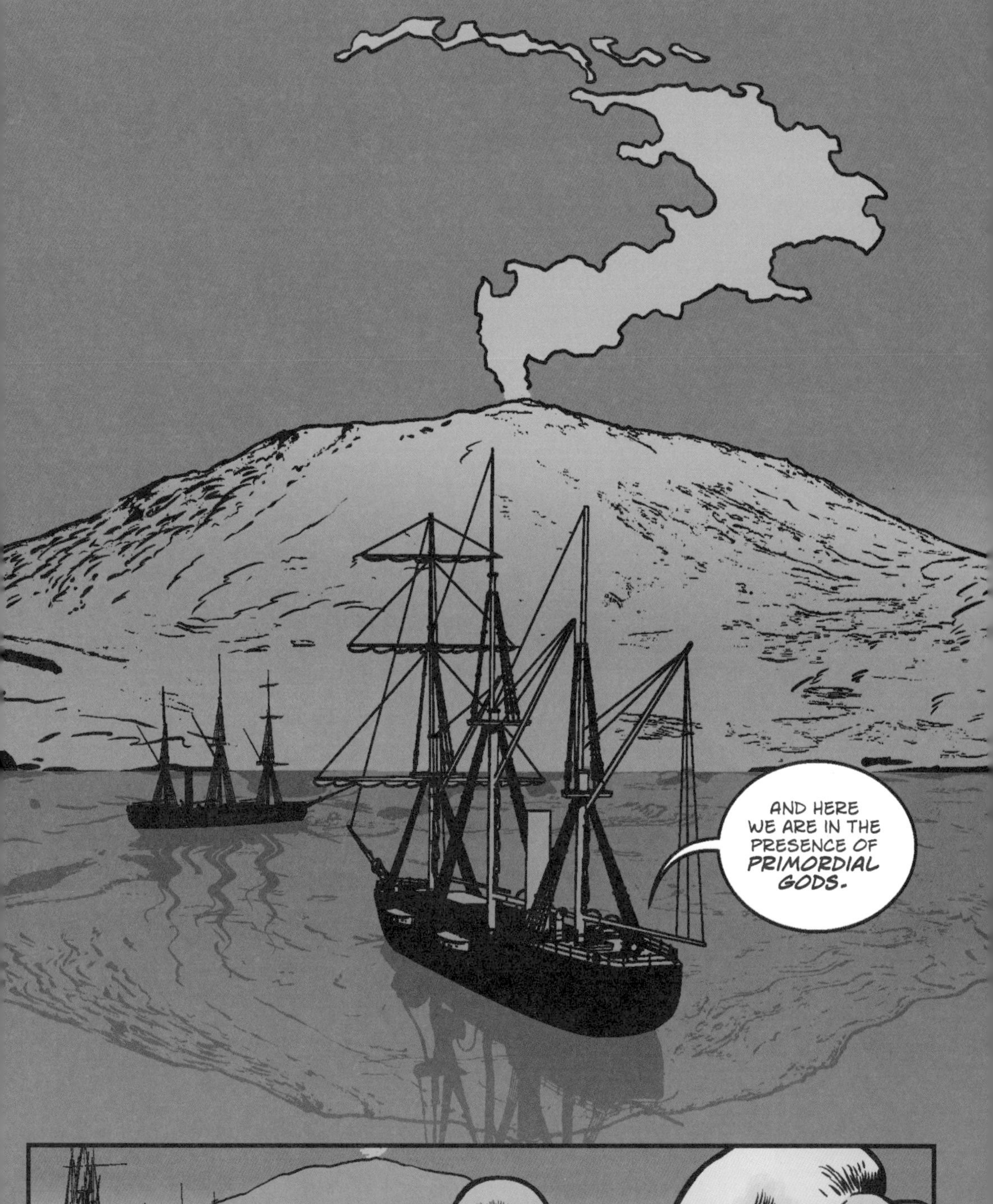
AND HERE WE ARE IN THE PRESENCE OF PRIMORDIAL GODS.

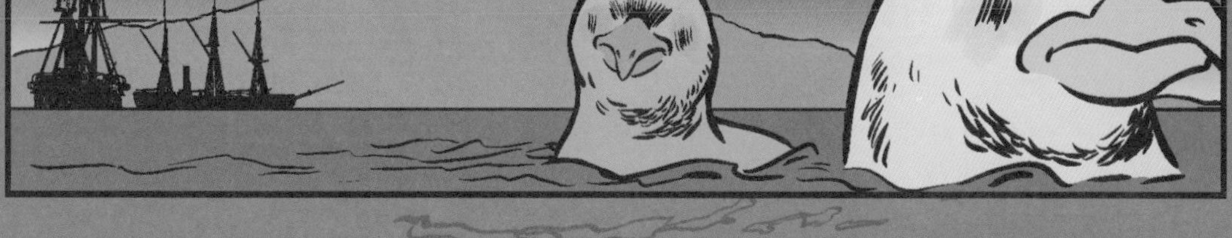

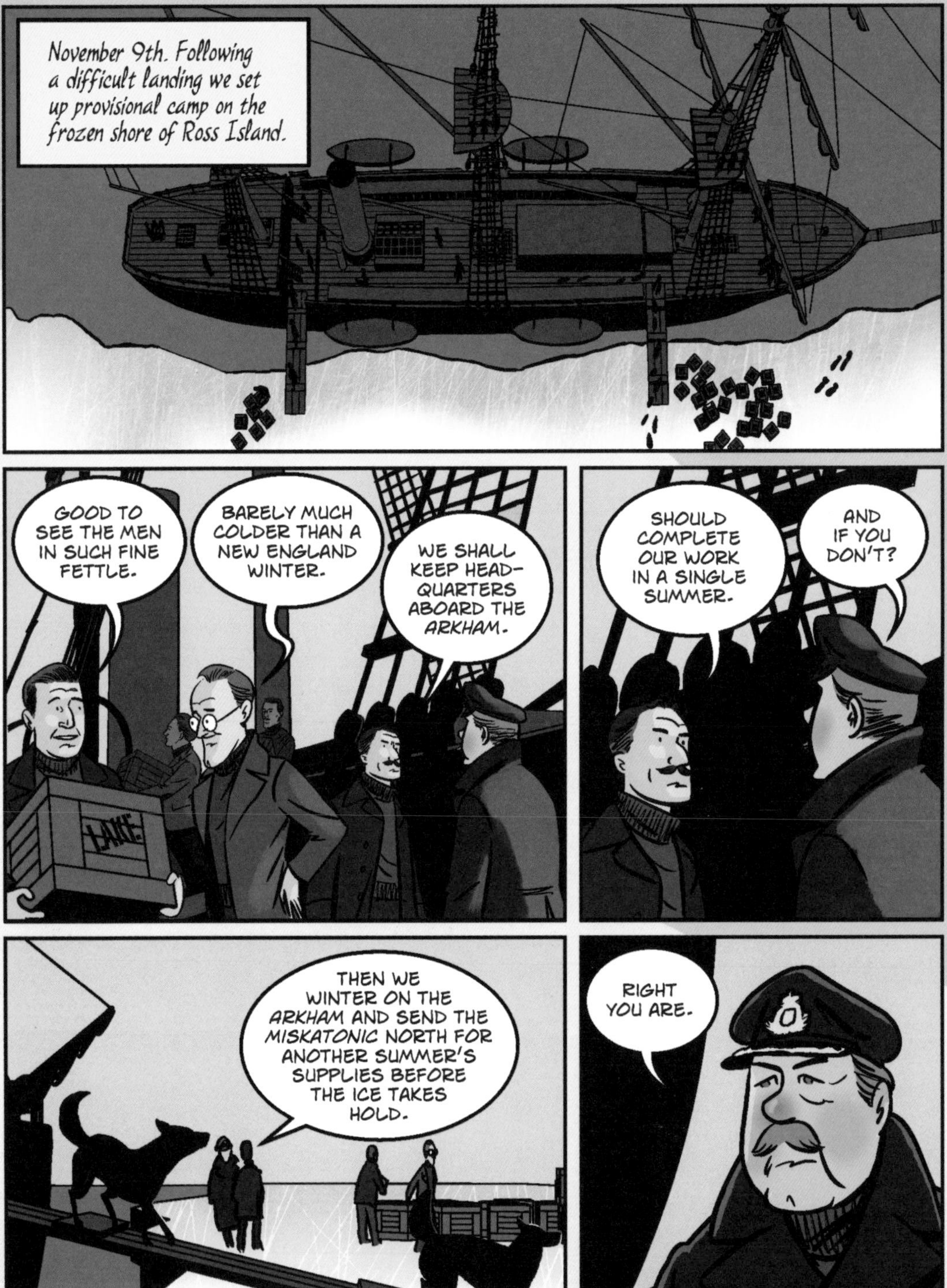
November 9th. Following a difficult landing we set up provisional camp on the frozen shore of Ross Island.
GOOD TO SEE THE MEN IN SUCH FINE FETTLE.
BARELY MUCH COLDER THAN A NEW ENGLAND WINTER.
WE SHALL KEEP HEAD-QUARTERS ABOARD THE *ARKHAM*.
SHOULD COMPLETE OUR WORK IN A SINGLE SUMMER.
AND IF YOU DON'T?
THEN WE WINTER ON THE *ARKHAM* AND SEND THE *MISKATONIC* NORTH FOR ANOTHER SUMMER'S SUPPLIES BEFORE THE ICE TAKES HOLD.
RIGHT YOU ARE.

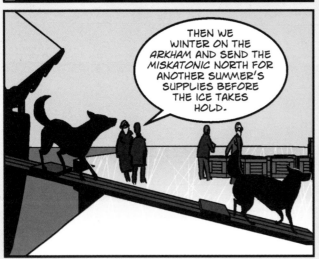

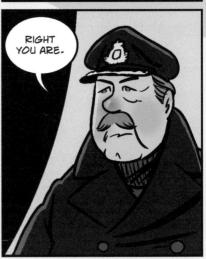

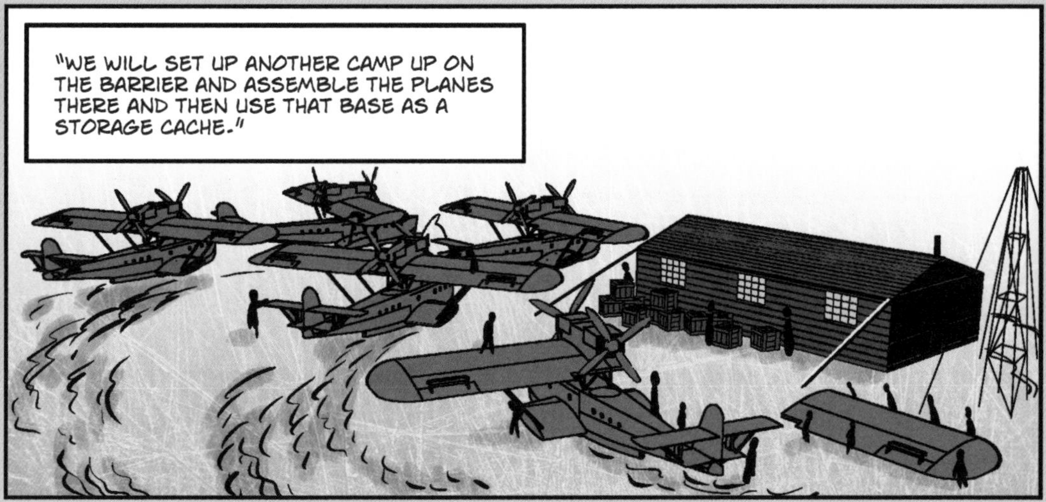
"WE WILL SET UP ANOTHER CAMP UP ON THE BARRIER AND ASSEMBLE THE PLANES THERE AND THEN USE THAT BASE AS A STORAGE CACHE."

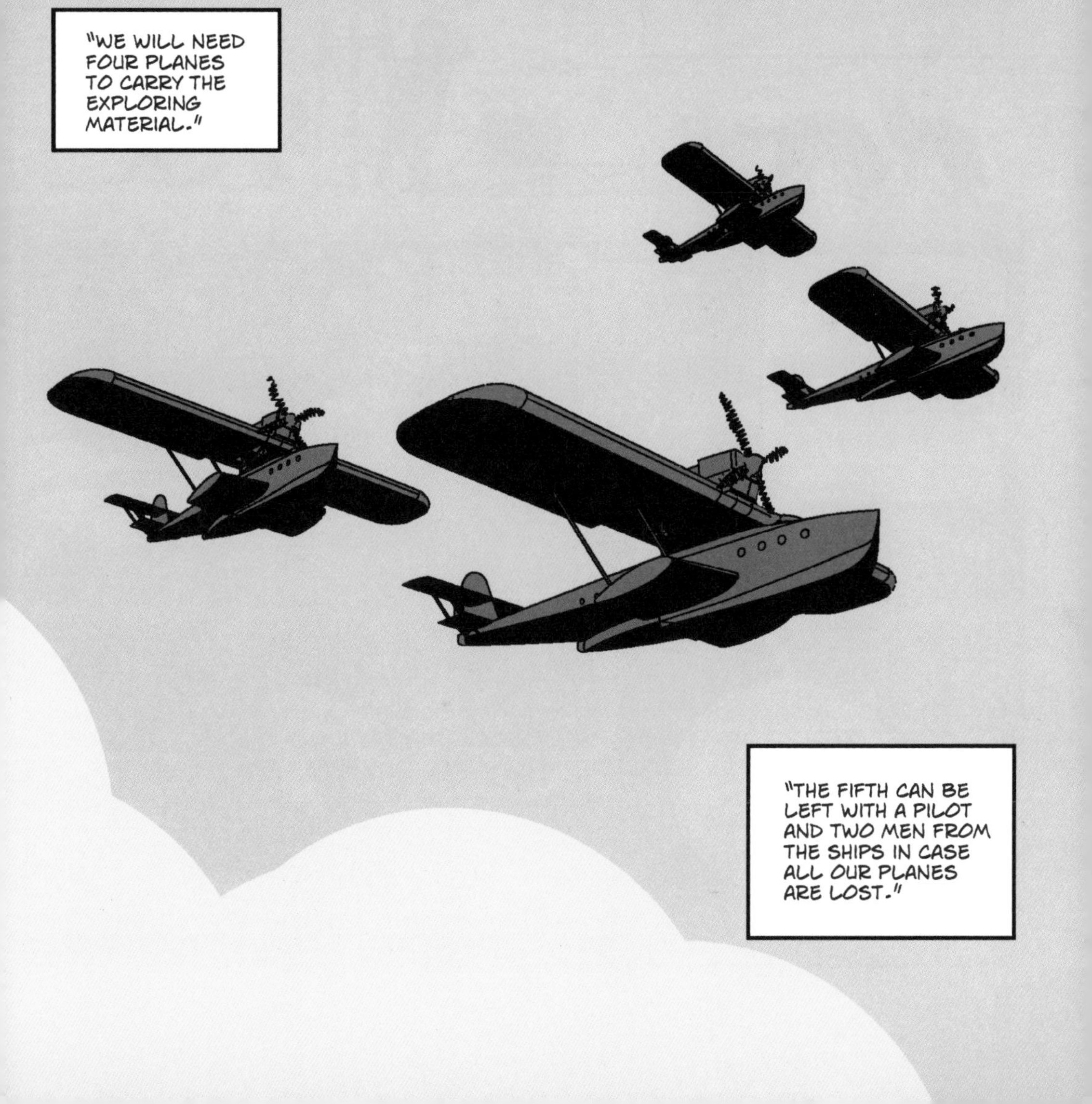
"WE WILL NEED FOUR PLANES TO CARRY THE EXPLORING MATERIAL."
"THE FIFTH CAN BE LEFT WITH A PILOT AND TWO MEN FROM THE SHIPS IN CASE ALL OUR PLANES ARE LOST."

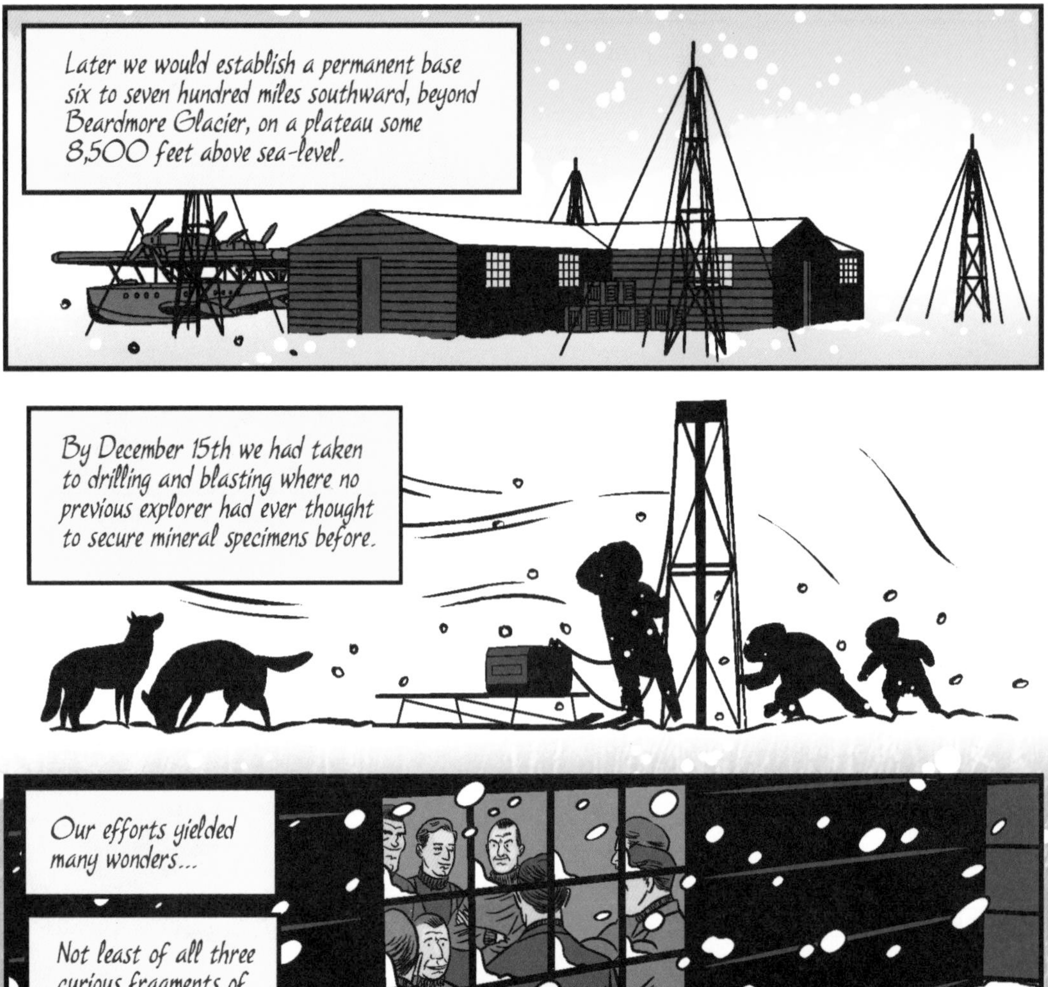

Later we would establish a permanent base six to seven hundred miles southward, beyond Beardmore Glacier, on a plateau some 8,500 feet above sea-level.
By December 15th we had taken to drilling and blasting where no previous explorer had ever thought to secure mineral specimens before.
Our efforts yielded many wonders...
Not least of all three curious fragments of slate.
NOTICE THE QUEER TRIANGULAR, STRIATED MARKING.
POSSIBLY THE PRINT OF SOME LARGE, UNKNOWN ORGANISM OF CONSIDERABLY ADVANCED EVOLUTION.

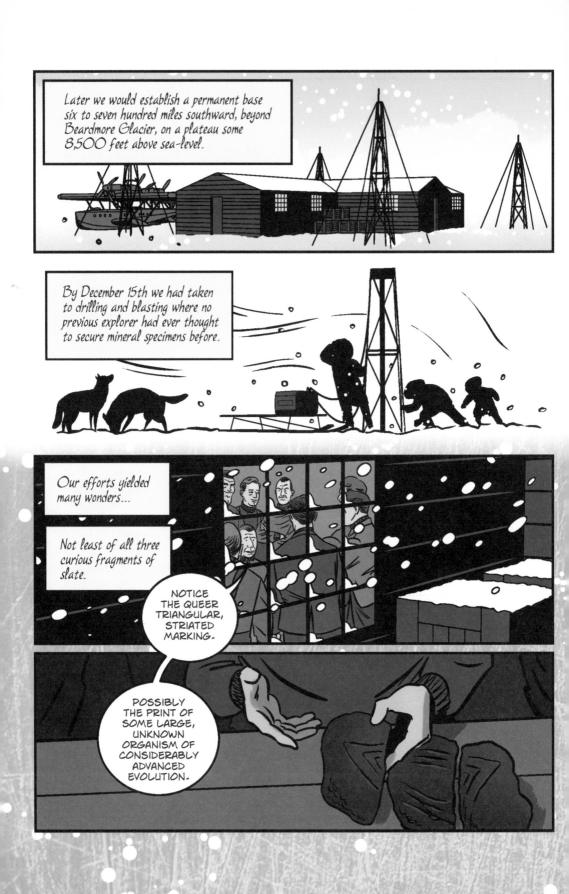

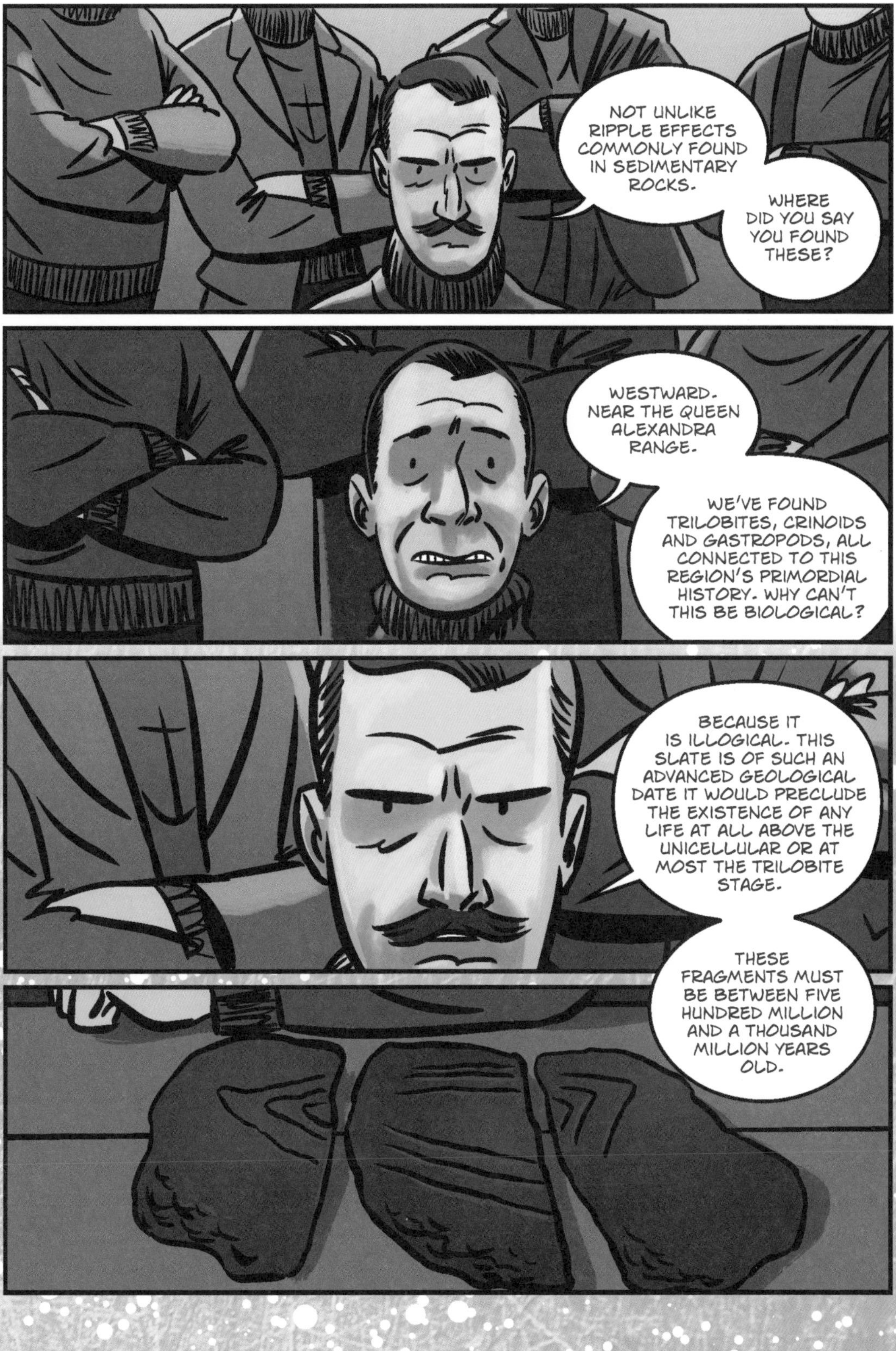
NOT UNLIKE RIPPLE EFFECTS COMMONLY FOUND IN SEDIMENTARY ROCKS.
WHERE DID YOU SAY YOU FOUND THESE?
WESTWARD. NEAR THE QUEEN ALEXANDRA RANGE.
WE'VE FOUND TRILOBITES, CRINOIDS AND GASTROPODS, ALL CONNECTED TO THIS REGION'S PRIMORDIAL HISTORY. WHY CAN'T THIS BE BIOLOGICAL?
BECAUSE IT IS ILLOGICAL. THIS SLATE IS OF SUCH AN ADVANCED GEOLOGICAL DATE IT WOULD PRECLUDE THE EXISTENCE OF ANY LIFE AT ALL ABOVE THE UNICELLULAR OR AT MOST THE TRILOBITE STAGE.
THESE FRAGMENTS MUST BE BETWEEN FIVE HUNDRED MILLION AND A THOUSAND MILLION YEARS OLD.

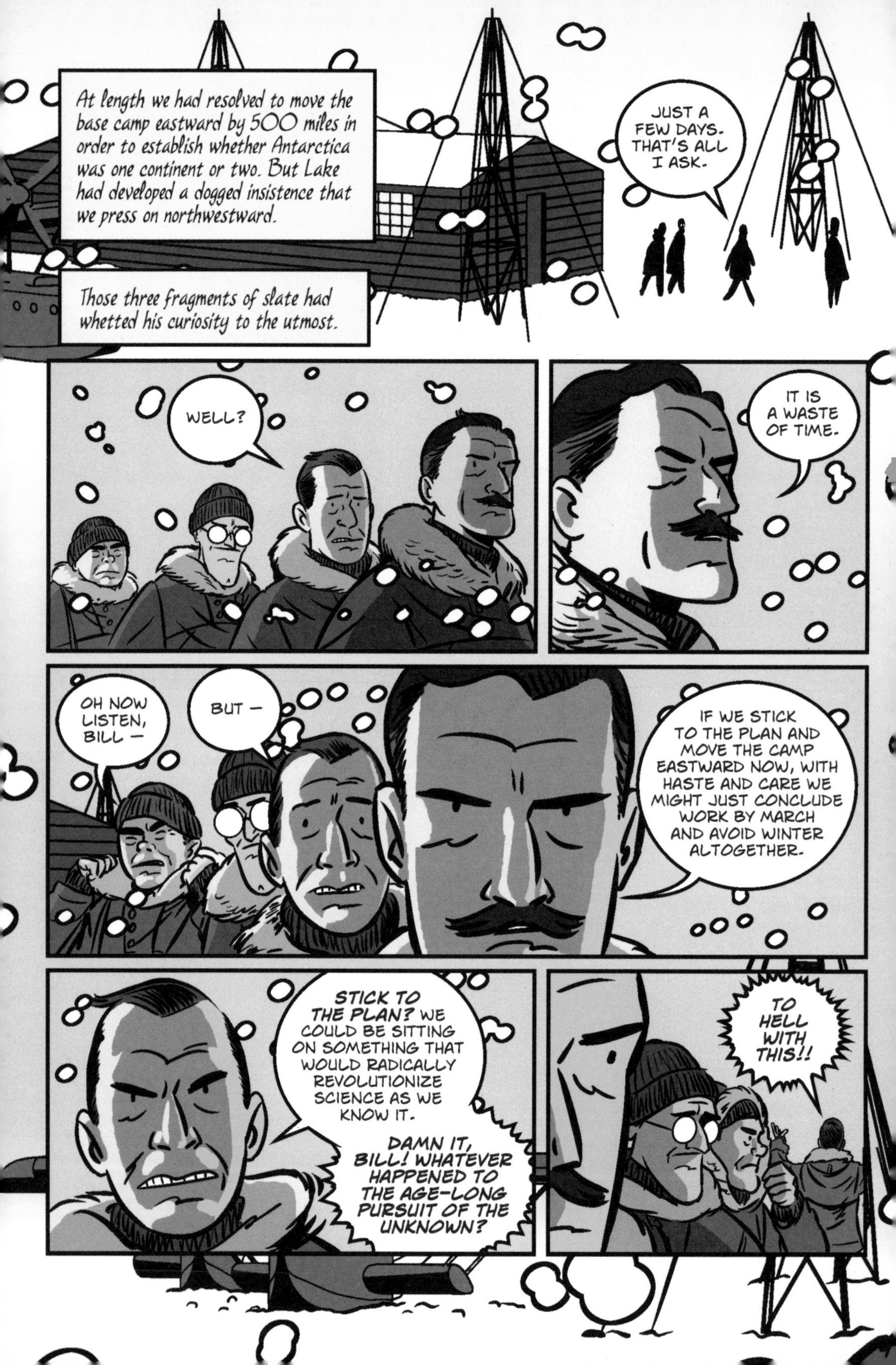
At length we had resolved to move the base camp eastward by 500 miles in order to establish whether Antarctica was one continent or two. But Lake had developed a dogged insistence that we press on northwestward.
Those three fragments of slate had whetted his curiosity to the utmost.
JUST A FEW DAYS. THAT'S ALL I ASK.
WELL?
IT IS A WASTE OF TIME.
OH NOW LISTEN, BILL —
BUT —
IF WE STICK TO THE PLAN AND MOVE THE CAMP EASTWARD NOW, WITH HASTE AND CARE WE MIGHT JUST CONCLUDE WORK BY MARCH AND AVOID WINTER ALTOGETHER.
STICK TO THE PLAN? WE COULD BE SITTING ON SOMETHING THAT WOULD RADICALLY REVOLUTIONIZE SCIENCE AS WE KNOW IT.
DAMN IT, BILL! WHATEVER HAPPENED TO THE AGE-LONG PURSUIT OF THE UNKNOWN?
TO HELL WITH THIS!!

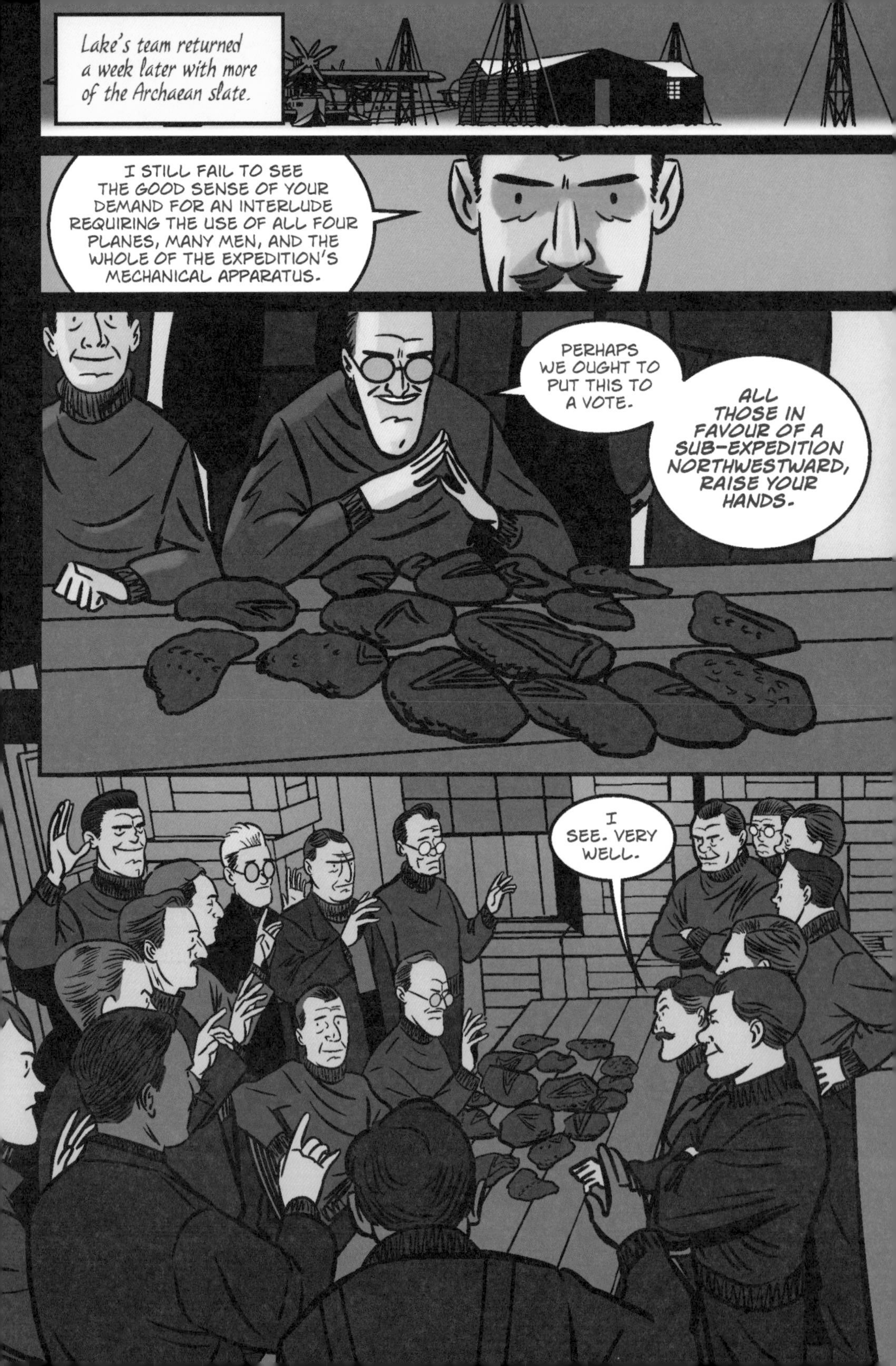
Lake's team returned a week later with more of the Archaean slate.
I STILL FAIL TO SEE THE GOOD SENSE OF YOUR DEMAND FOR AN INTERLUDE REQUIRING THE USE OF ALL FOUR PLANES, MANY MEN, AND THE WHOLE OF THE EXPEDITION'S MECHANICAL APPARATUS.
PERHAPS WE OUGHT TO PUT THIS TO A VOTE.
ALL THOSE IN FAVOUR OF A SUB-EXPEDITION NORTHWESTWARD, RAISE YOUR HANDS.
I SEE. VERY WELL.

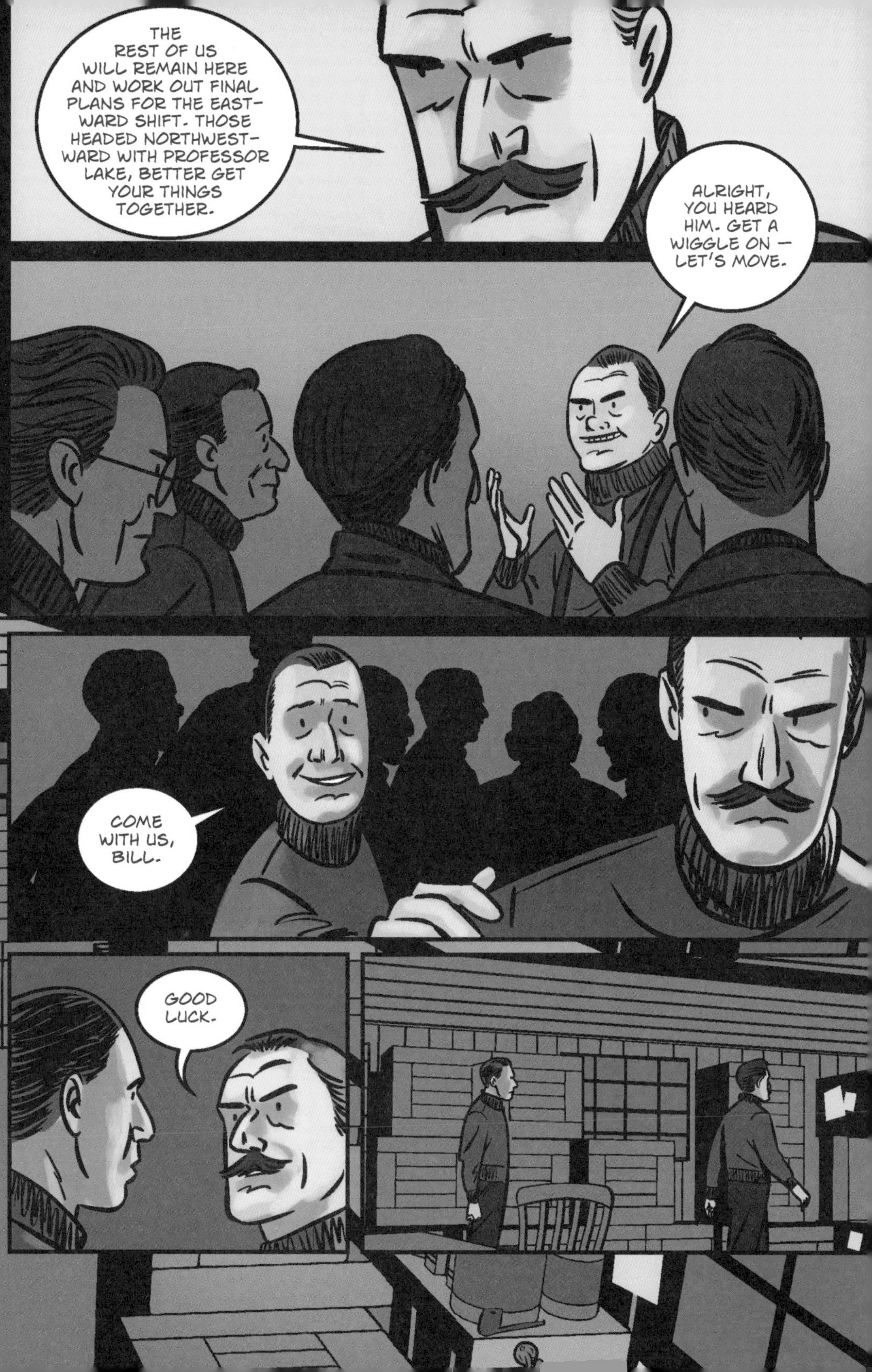
THE REST OF US WILL REMAIN HERE AND WORK OUT FINAL PLANS FOR THE EAST-WARD SHIFT. THOSE HEADED NORTHWEST-WARD WITH PROFESSOR LAKE, BETTER GET YOUR THINGS TOGETHER.
ALRIGHT, YOU HEARD HIM. GET A WIGGLE ON — LET'S MOVE.
COME WITH US, BILL.
GOOD LUCK.

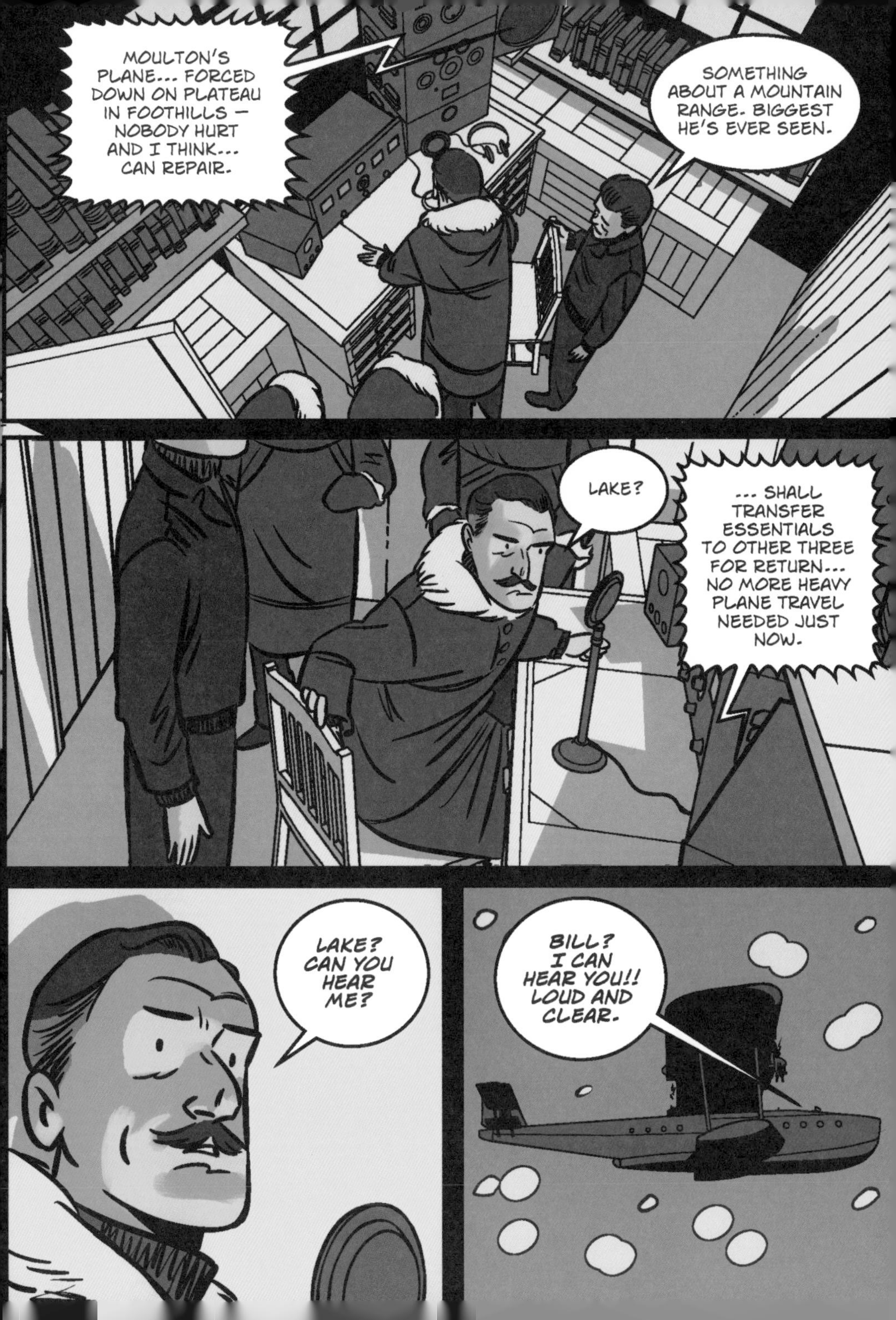
MOULTON'S PLANE... FORCED DOWN ON PLATEAU IN FOOTHILLS — NOBODY HURT AND I THINK... CAN REPAIR.
SOMETHING ABOUT A MOUNTAIN RANGE. BIGGEST HE'S EVER SEEN.
LAKE?
... SHALL TRANSFER ESSENTIALS TO OTHER THREE FOR RETURN... NO MORE HEAVY PLANE TRAVEL NEEDED JUST NOW.
LAKE? CAN YOU HEAR ME?
BILL? I CAN HEAR YOU!! LOUD AND CLEAR.

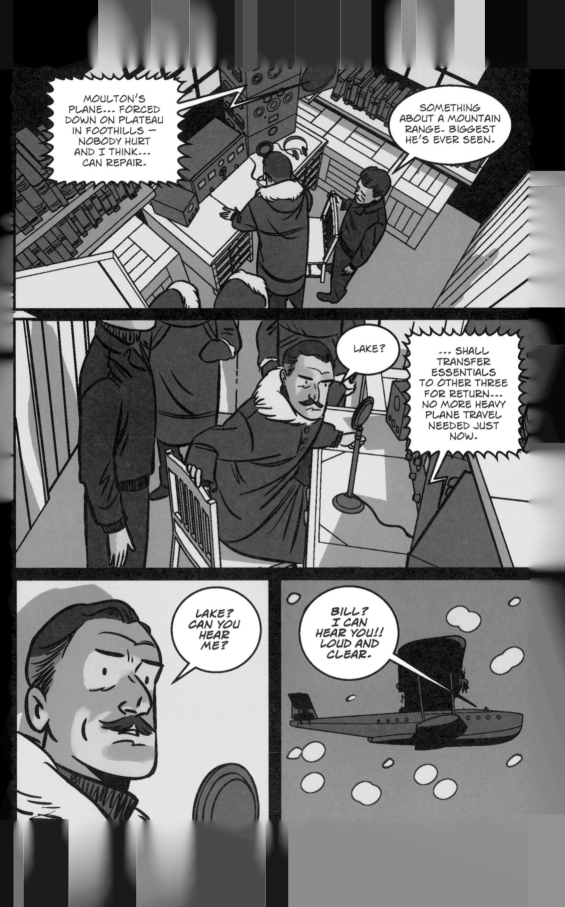

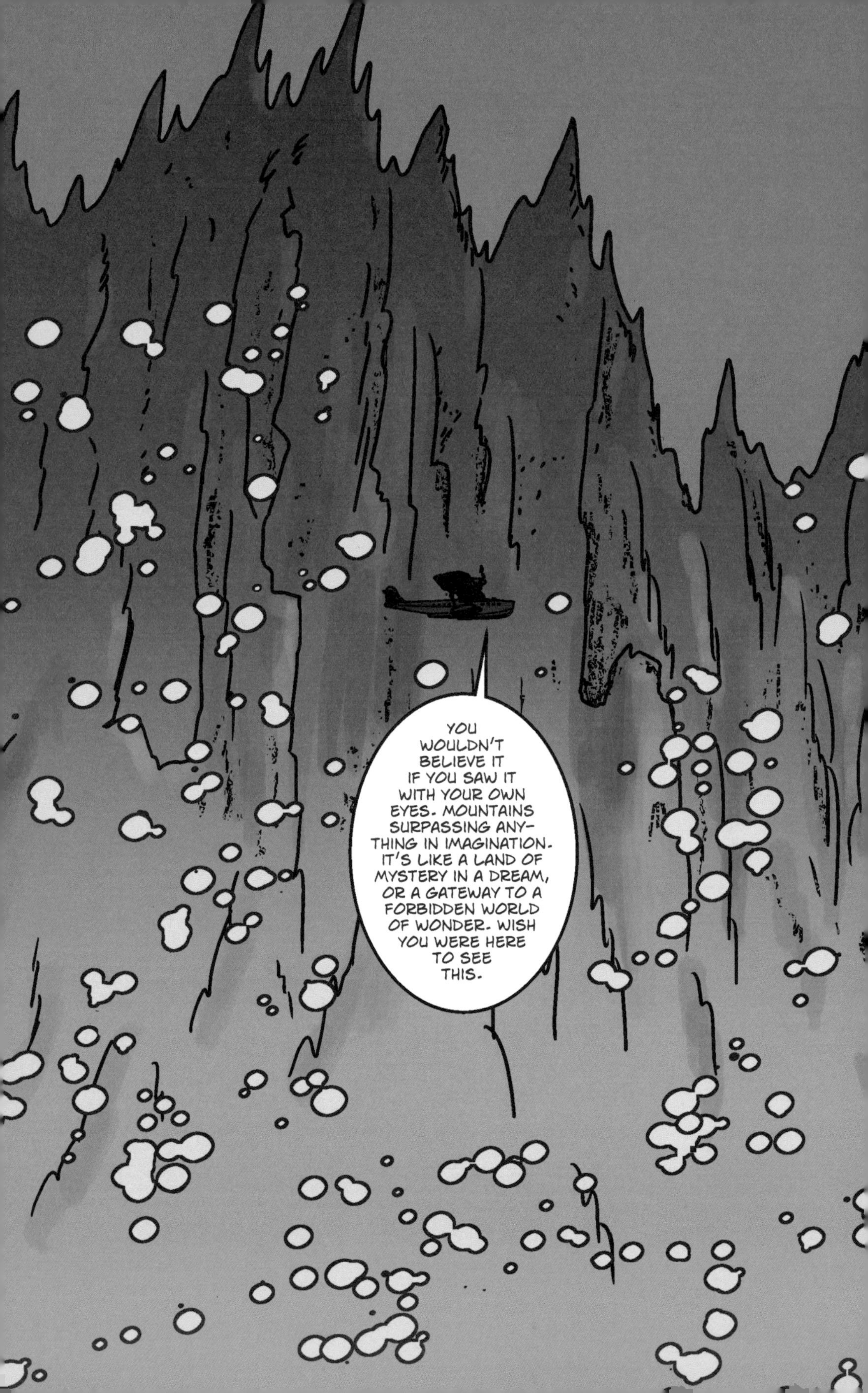
YOU WOULDN'T BELIEVE IT IF YOU SAW IT WITH YOUR OWN EYES. MOUNTAINS SURPASSING ANY-THING IN IMAGINATION. IT'S LIKE A LAND OF MYSTERY IN A DREAM, OR A GATEWAY TO A FORBIDDEN WORLD OF WONDER. WISH YOU WERE HERE TO SEE THIS.

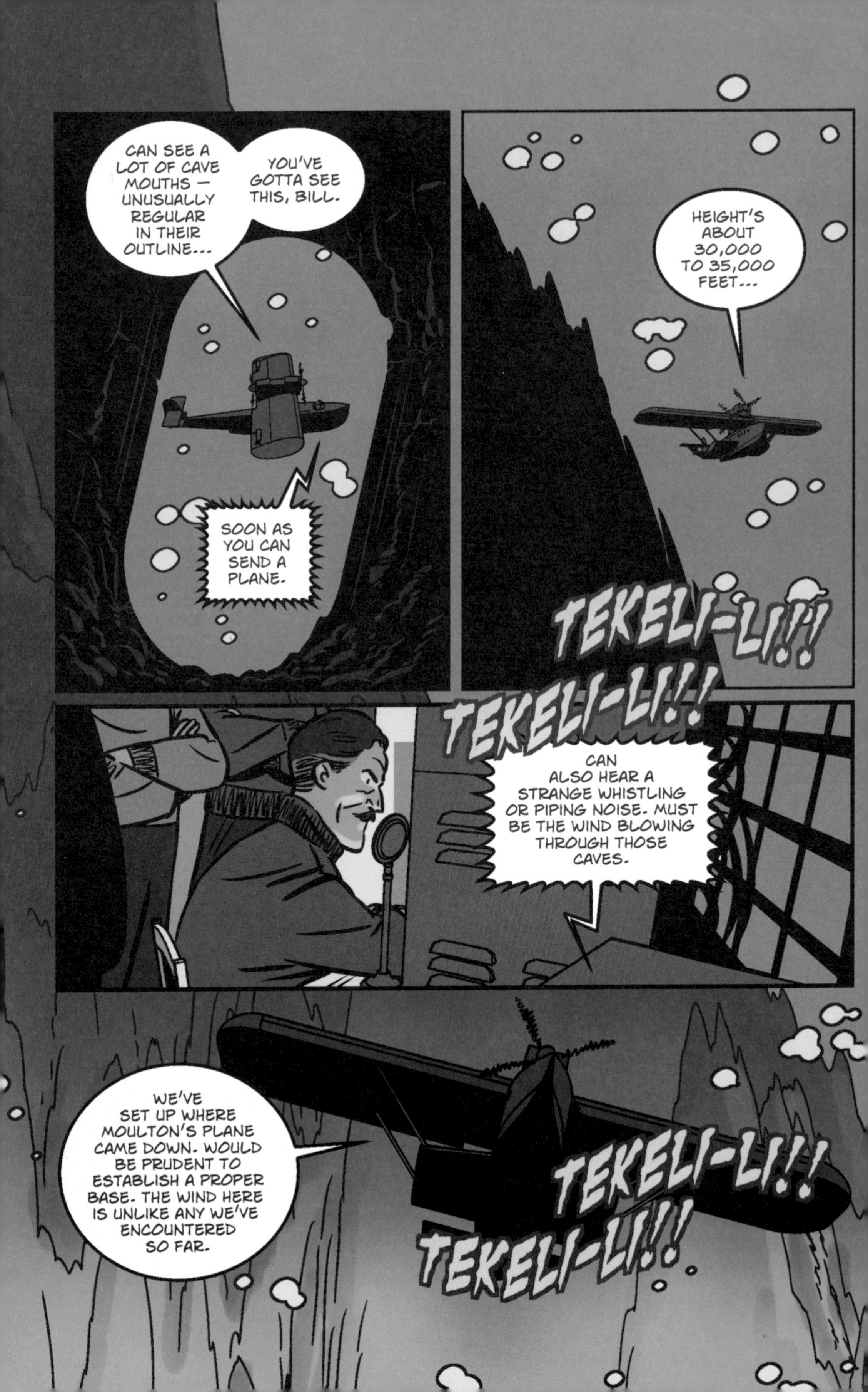
CAN SEE A LOT OF CAVE MOUTHS — UNUSUALLY REGULAR IN THEIR OUTLINE...
YOU'VE GOTTA SEE THIS, BILL.
SOON AS YOU CAN SEND A PLANE.
HEIGHT'S ABOUT 30,000 TO 35,000 FEET...
TEKELI-LI!!
TEKELI-LI!!
CAN ALSO HEAR A STRANGE WHISTLING OR PIPING NOISE. MUST BE THE WIND BLOWING THROUGH THOSE CAVES.
WE'VE SET UP WHERE MOULTON'S PLANE CAME DOWN. WOULD BE PRUDENT TO ESTABLISH A PROPER BASE. THE WIND HERE IS UNLIKE ANY WE'VE ENCOUNTERED SO FAR.
TEKELI-LI!!
TEKELI-LI!!

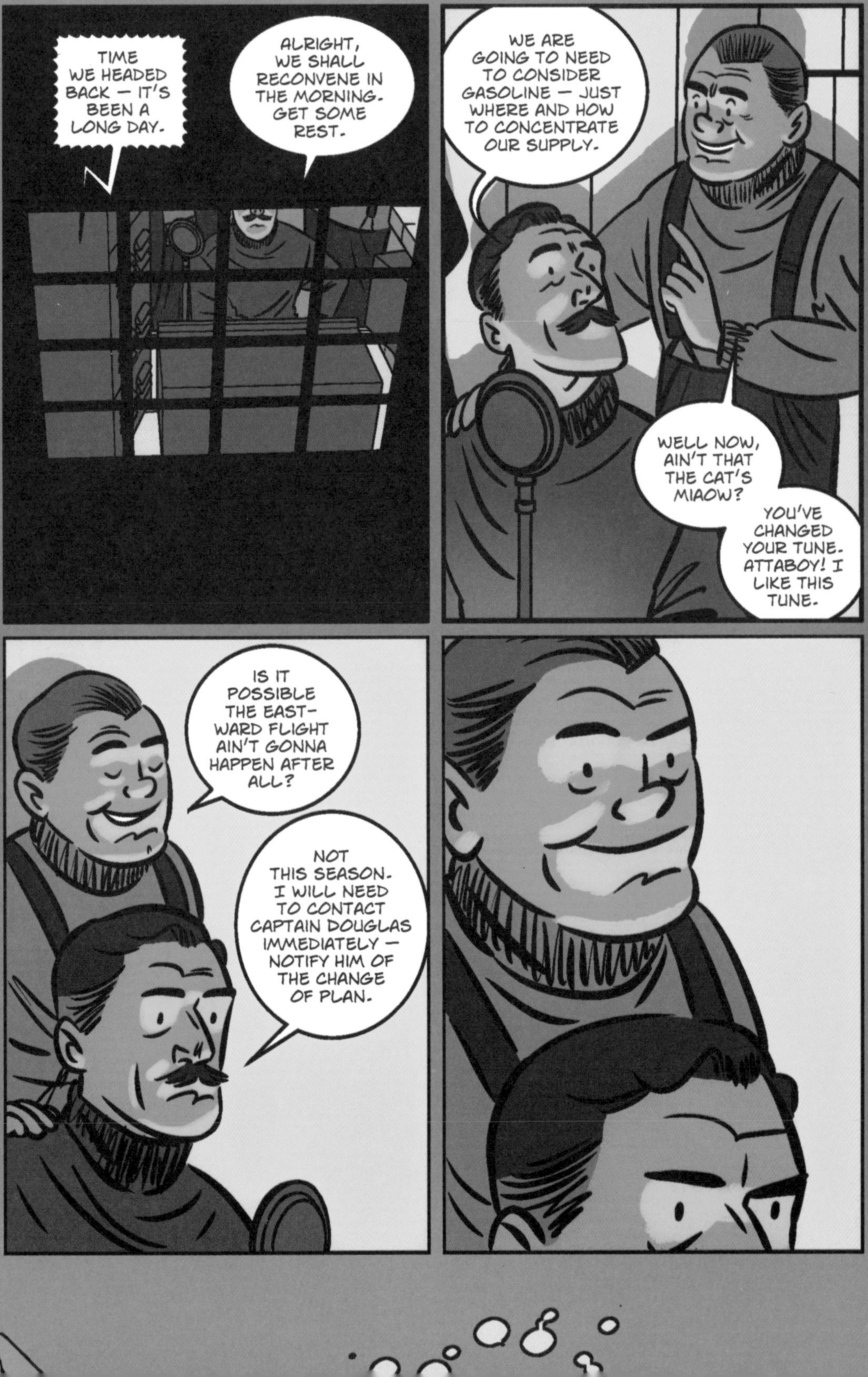
TIME WE HEADED BACK — IT'S BEEN A LONG DAY.
ALRIGHT, WE SHALL RECONVENE IN THE MORNING. GET SOME REST.
WE ARE GOING TO NEED TO CONSIDER GASOLINE — JUST WHERE AND HOW TO CONCENTRATE OUR SUPPLY.
WELL NOW, AIN'T THAT THE CAT'S MIAOW?
YOU'VE CHANGED YOUR TUNE. ATTABOY! I LIKE THIS TUNE.
IS IT POSSIBLE THE EAST-WARD FLIGHT AIN'T GONNA HAPPEN AFTER ALL?
NOT THIS SEASON. I WILL NEED TO CONTACT CAPTAIN DOUGLAS IMMEDIATELY — NOTIFY HIM OF THE CHANGE OF PLAN.

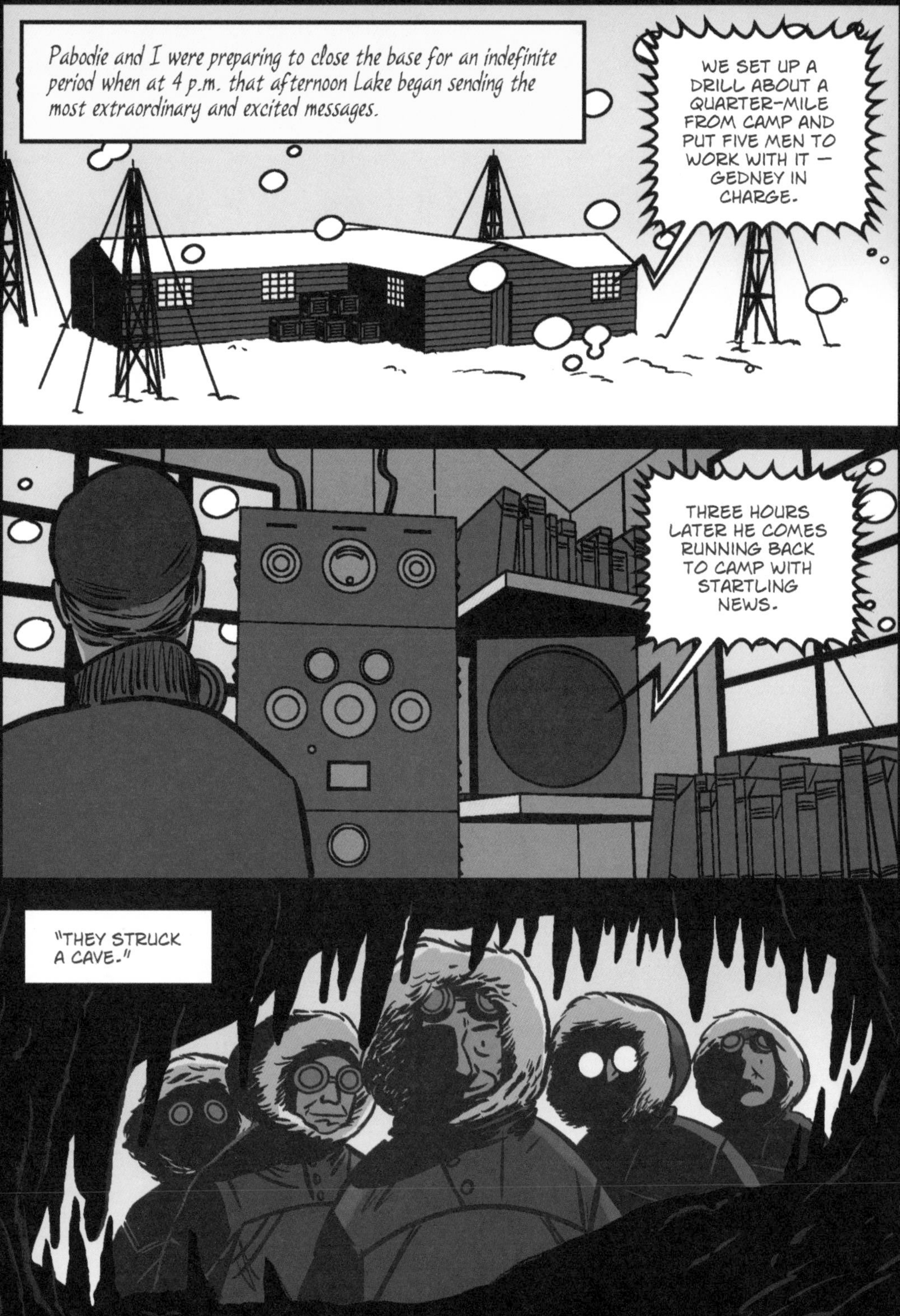
Pabodie and I were preparing to close the base for an indefinite period when at 4 p.m. that afternoon Lake began sending the most extraordinary and excited messages.
WE SET UP A DRILL ABOUT A QUARTER-MILE FROM CAMP AND PUT FIVE MEN TO WORK WITH IT — GEDNEY IN CHARGE.
THREE HOURS LATER HE COMES RUNNING BACK TO CAMP WITH STARTLING NEWS.
"THEY STRUCK A CAVE."

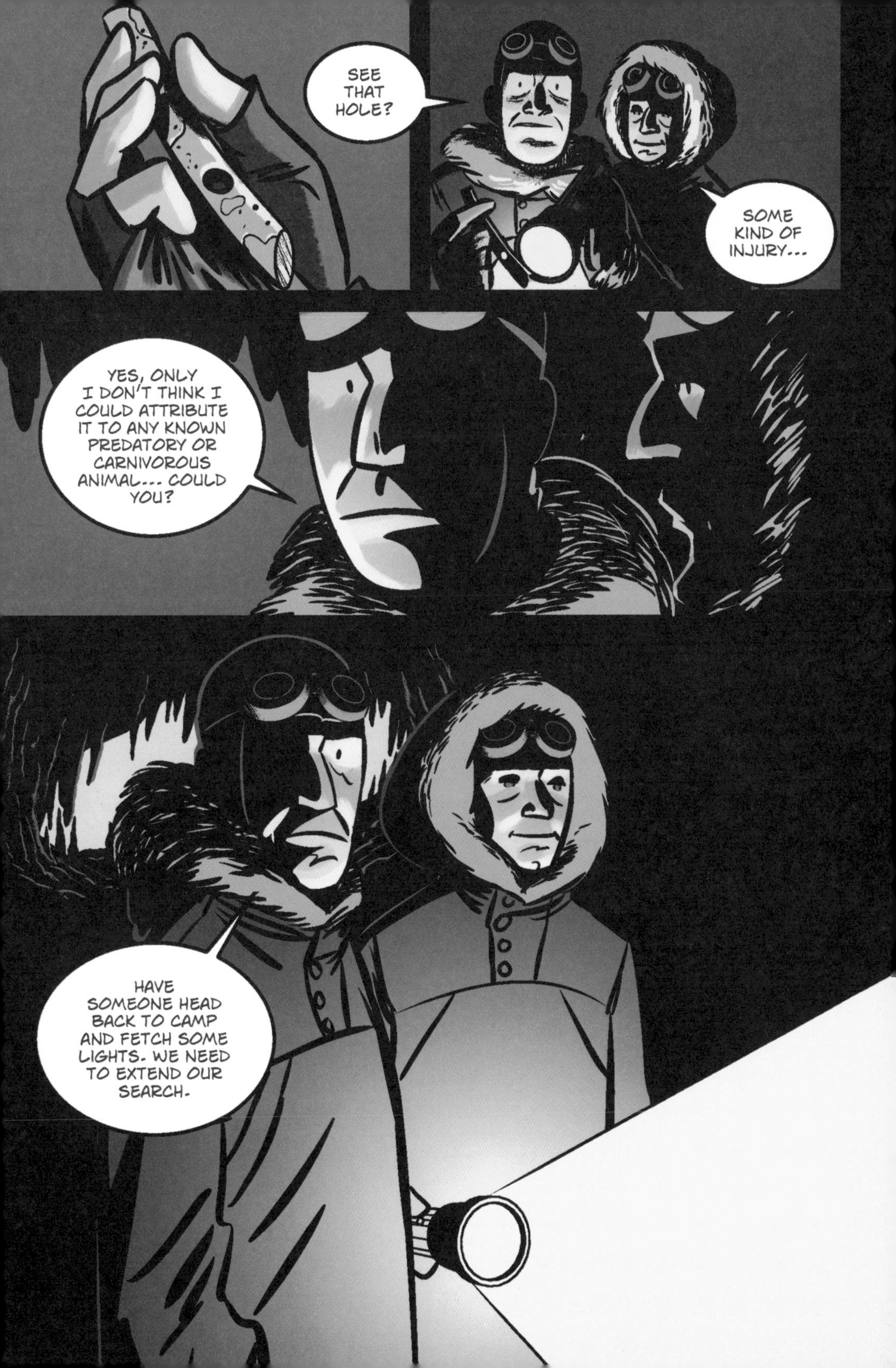
SEE THAT HOLE?
SOME KIND OF INJURY...
YES, ONLY I DON'T THINK I COULD ATTRIBUTE IT TO ANY KNOWN PREDATORY OR CARNIVOROUS ANIMAL... COULD YOU?
HAVE SOMEONE HEAD BACK TO CAMP AND FETCH SOME LIGHTS. WE NEED TO EXTEND OUR SEARCH.

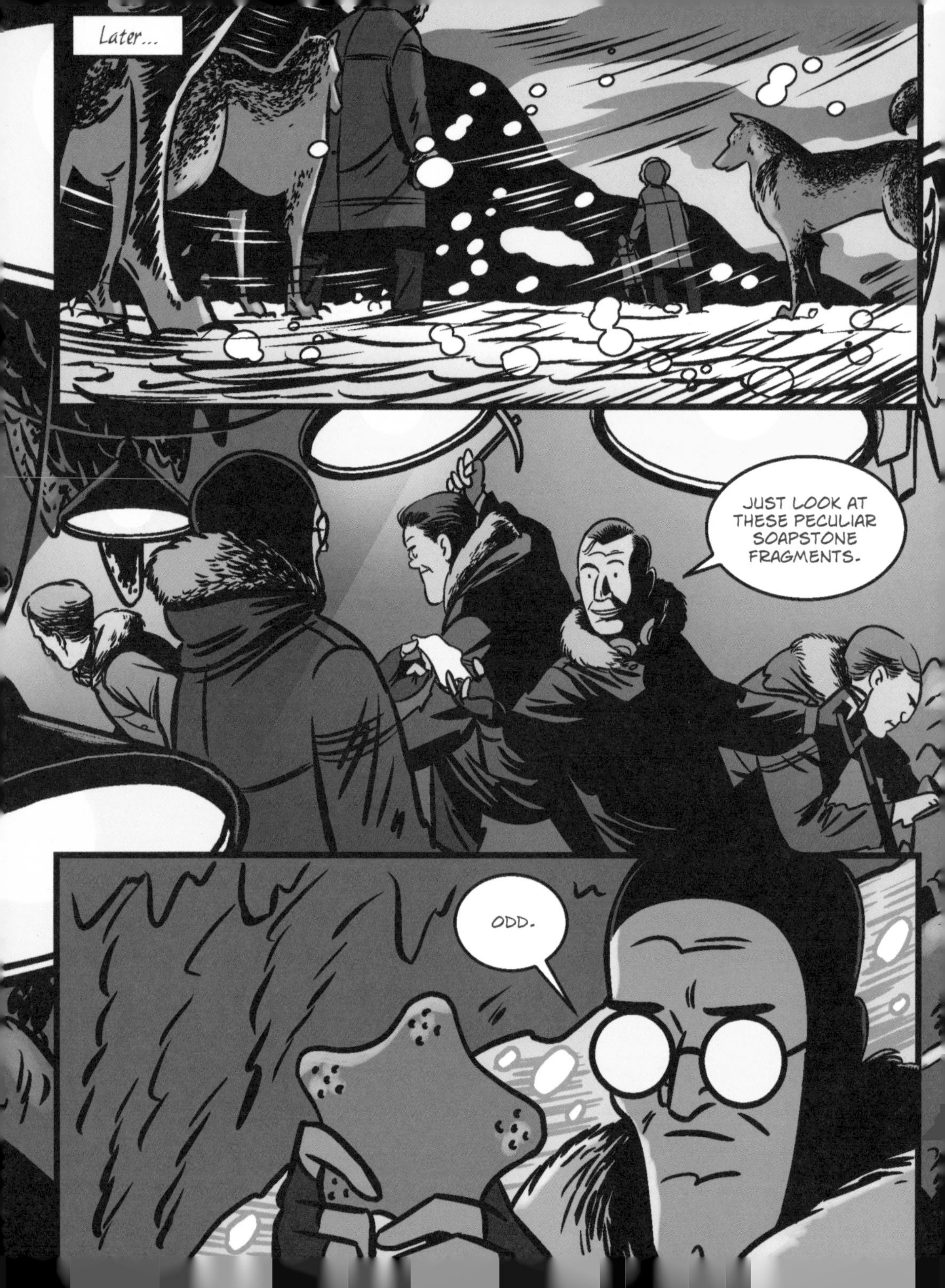
Later...
JUST LOOK AT THESE PECULIAR SOAPSTONE FRAGMENTS.
ODD.

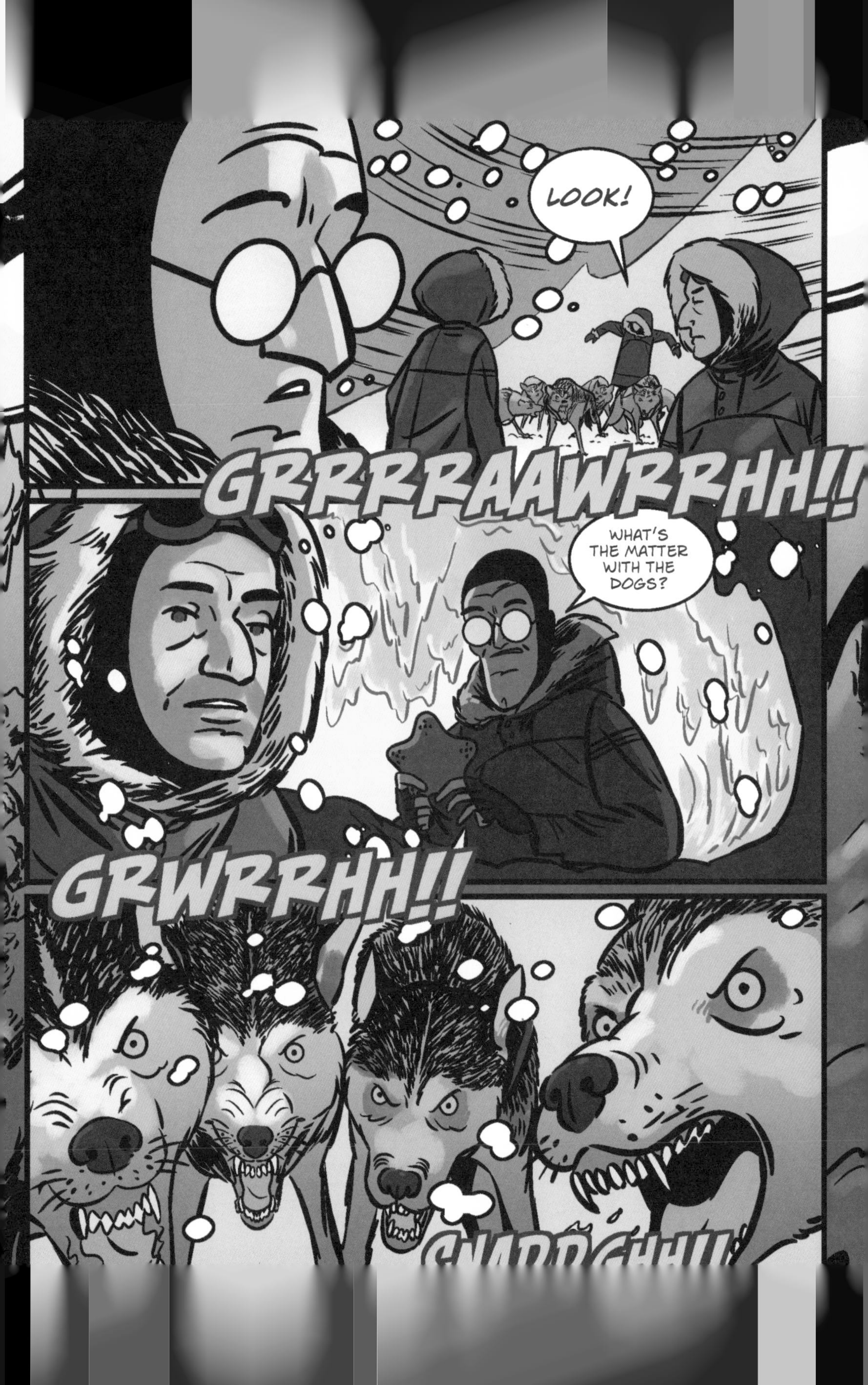
LOOK!
GRRRRAAWRRHH!!
WHAT'S THE MATTER WITH THE DOGS?
GRWRRHH!!

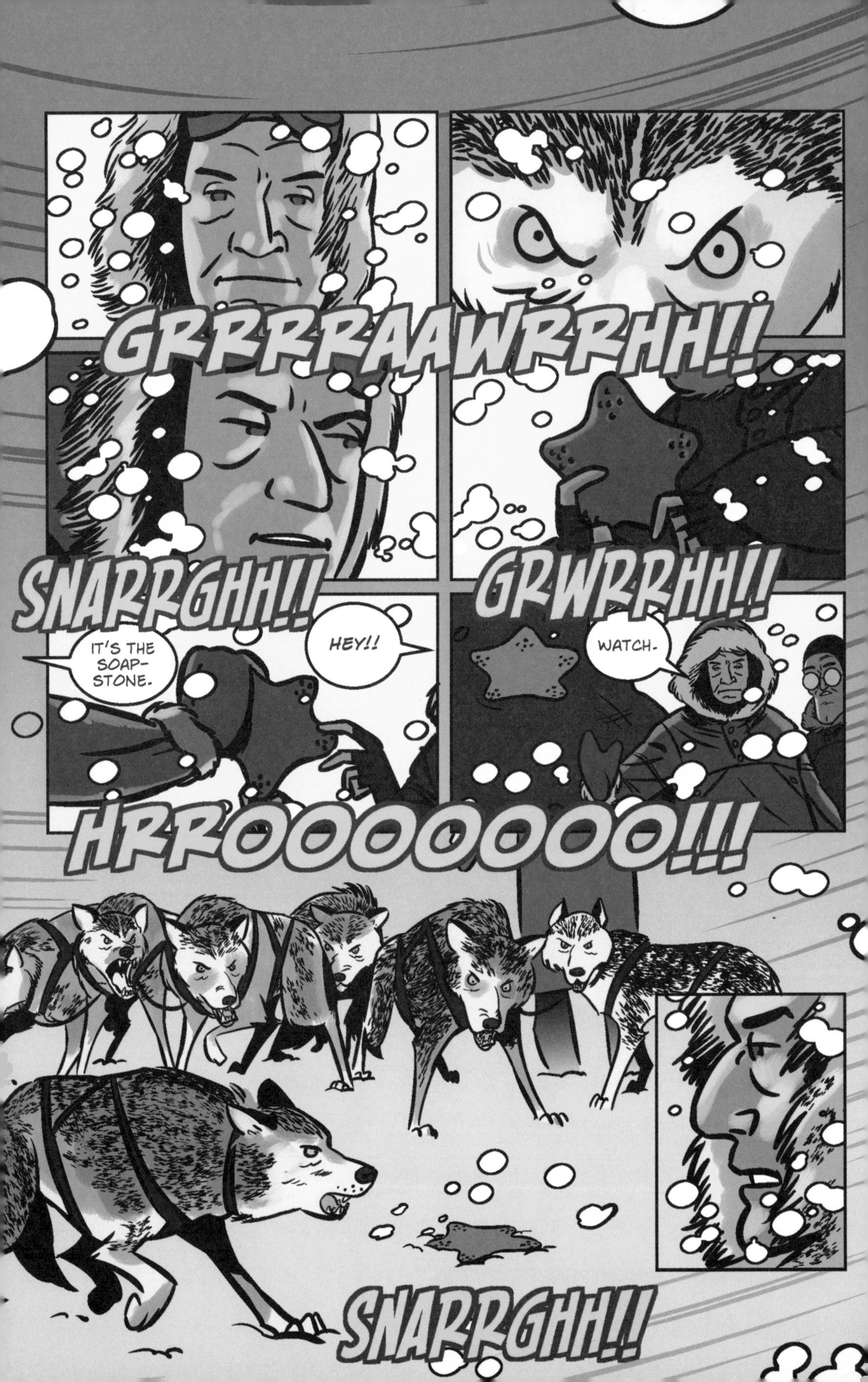
GRRRRAAWRRHH!!
SNARRGHH!!
GRWRRHH!!
IT'S THE SOAP-STONE.
HEY!!
WATCH.
HRROOOOOOOO!!!
SNARRGHH!!

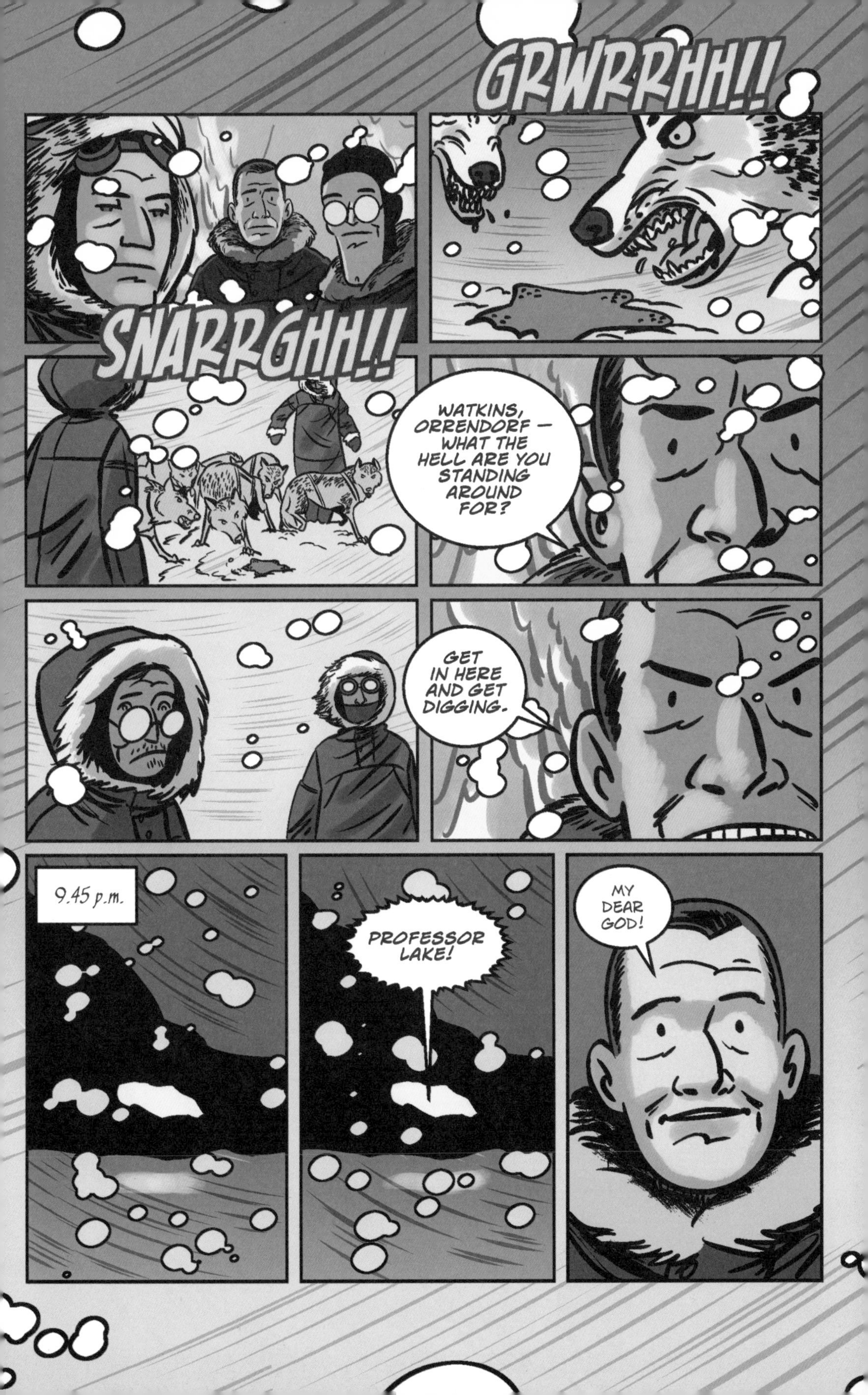
GRWRRHH!!
SNARRGHH!!
WATKINS, ORRENDORF — WHAT THE HELL ARE YOU STANDING AROUND FOR?
GET IN HERE AND GET DIGGING.
9.45 p.m.
PROFESSOR LAKE!
MY DEAR GOD!

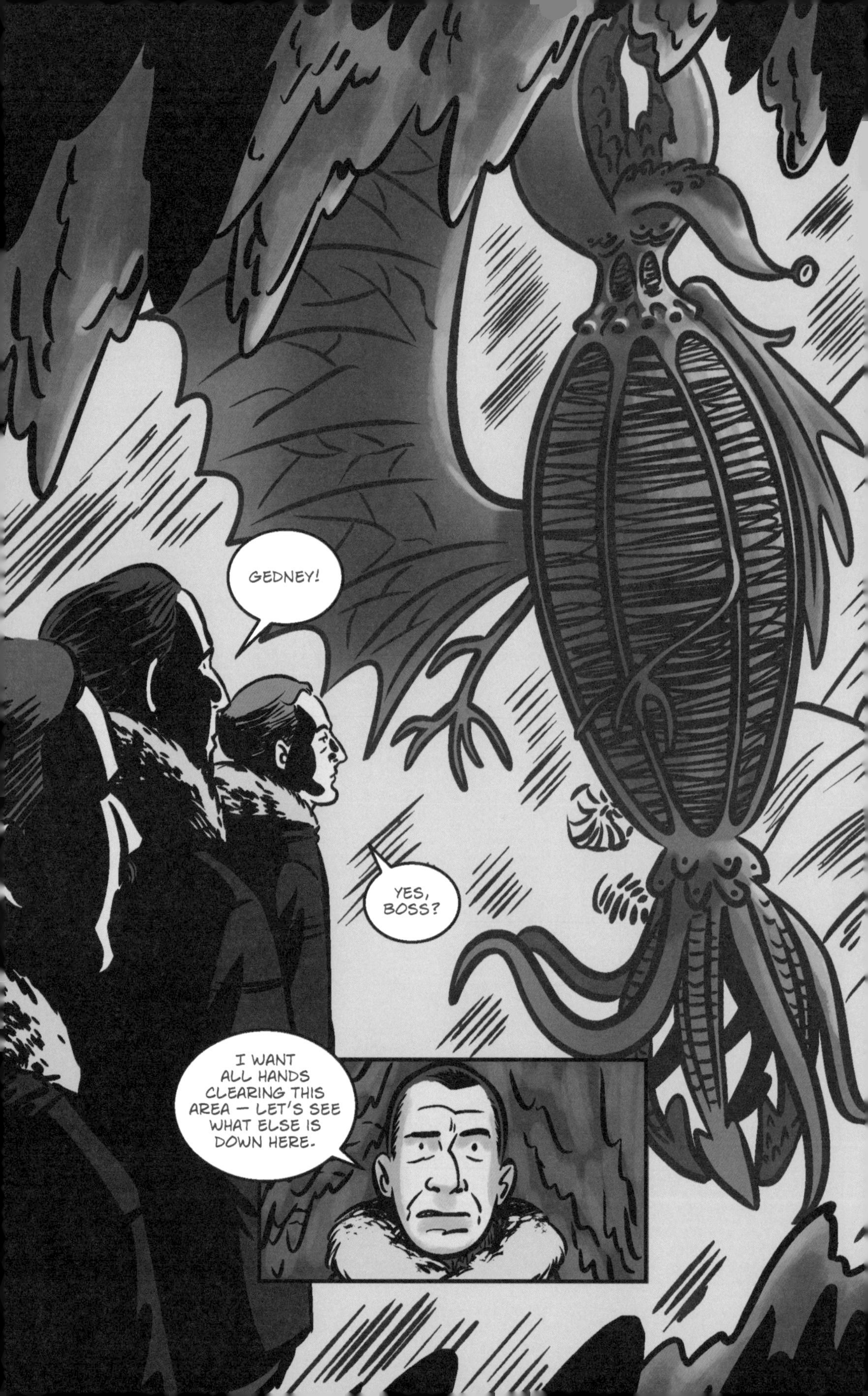
GEDNEY!
YES, BOSS?
I WANT ALL HANDS CLEARING THIS AREA — LET'S SEE WHAT ELSE IS DOWN HERE.

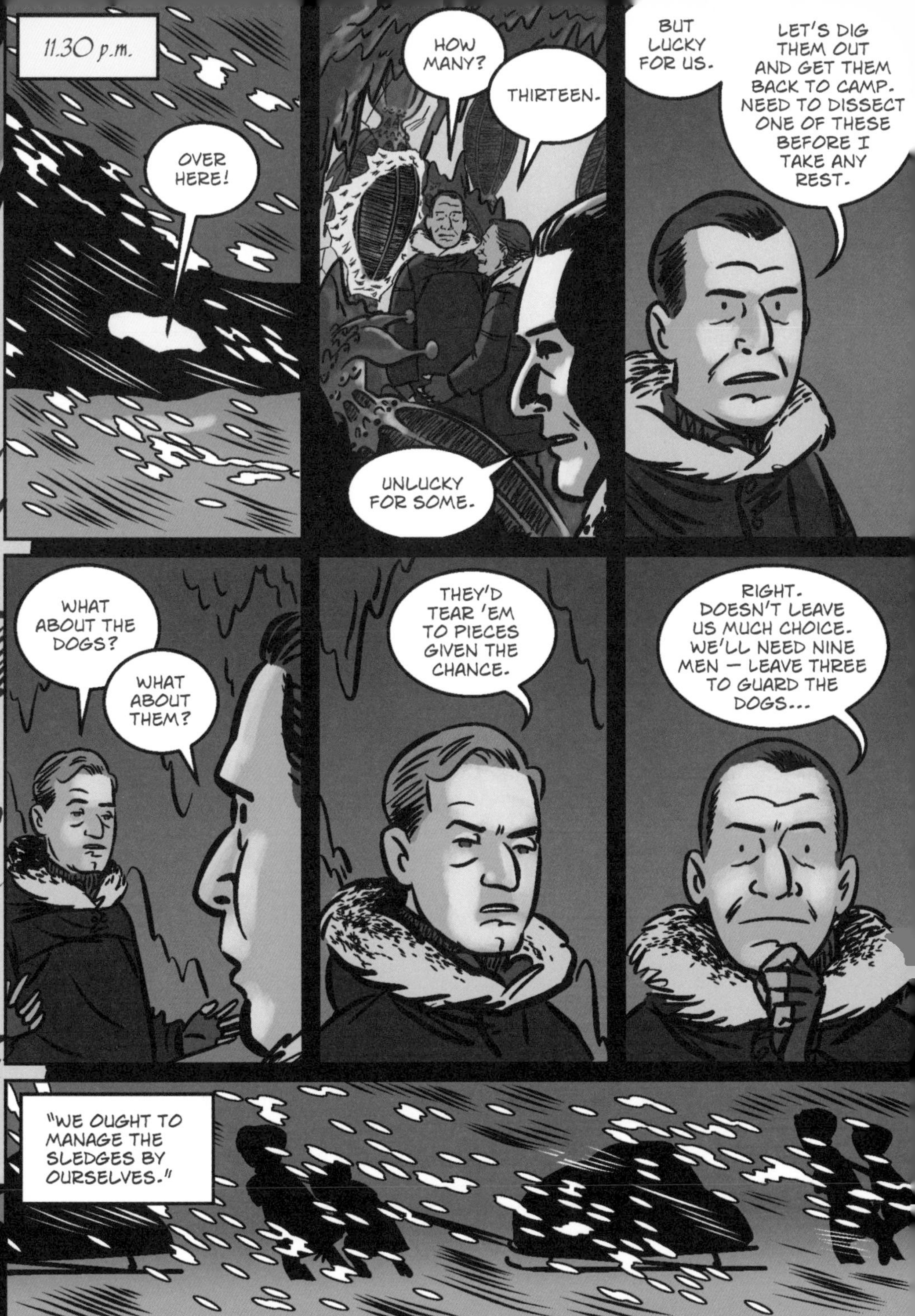
11.30 p.m.
OVER HERE!
HOW MANY?
THIRTEEN.
UNLUCKY FOR SOME.
BUT LUCKY FOR US.
LET'S DIG THEM OUT AND GET THEM BACK TO CAMP. NEED TO DISSECT ONE OF THESE BEFORE I TAKE ANY REST.
WHAT ABOUT THE DOGS?
WHAT ABOUT THEM?
THEY'D TEAR 'EM TO PIECES GIVEN THE CHANCE.
RIGHT. DOESN'T LEAVE US MUCH CHOICE. WE'LL NEED NINE MEN — LEAVE THREE TO GUARD THE DOGS...
"WE OUGHT TO MANAGE THE SLEDGES BY OURSELVES."

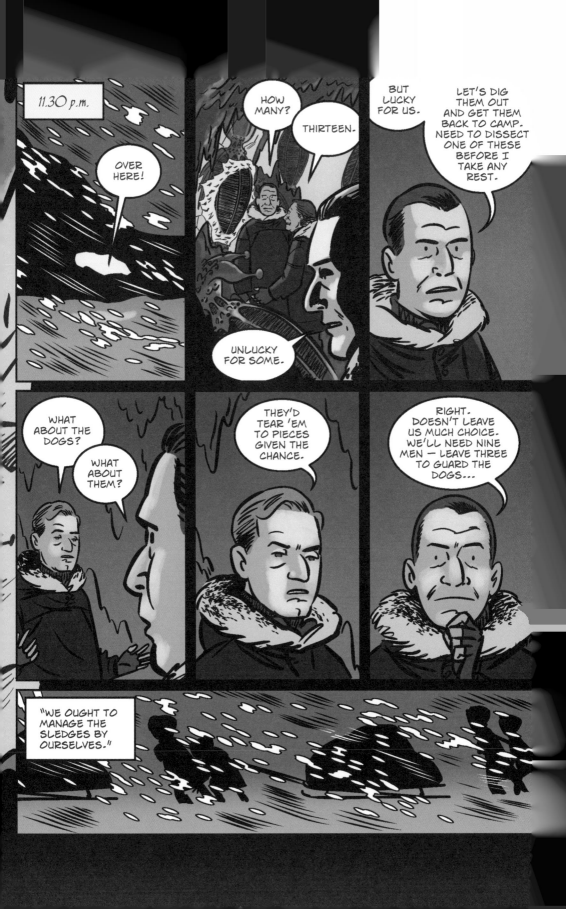

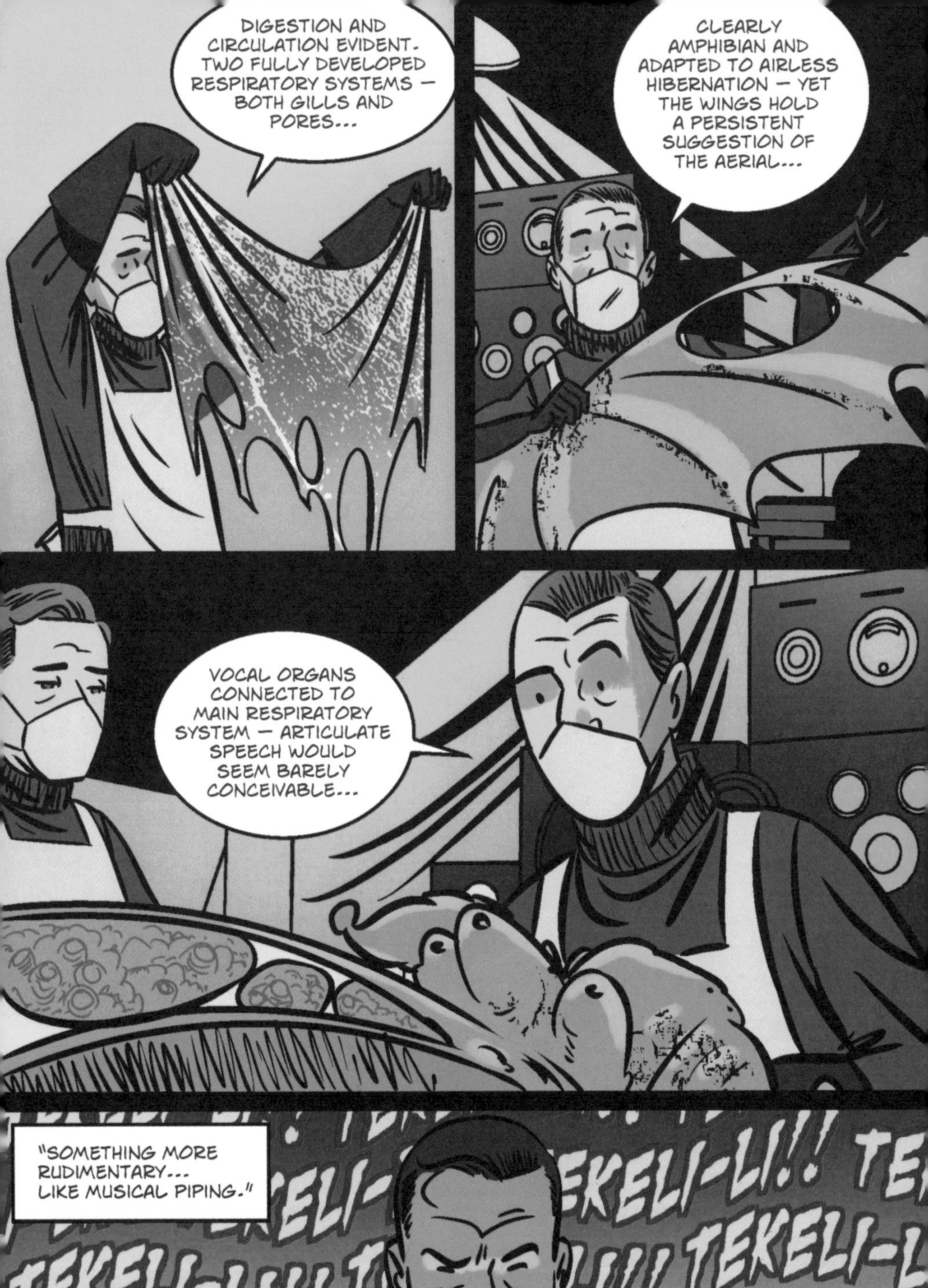
DIGESTION AND CIRCULATION EVIDENT. TWO FULLY DEVELOPED RESPIRATORY SYSTEMS — BOTH GILLS AND PORES...
CLEARLY AMPHIBIAN AND ADAPTED TO AIRLESS HIBERNATION — YET THE WINGS HOLD A PERSISTENT SUGGESTION OF THE AERIAL...
VOCAL ORGANS CONNECTED TO MAIN RESPIRATORY SYSTEM — ARTICULATE SPEECH WOULD SEEM BARELY CONCEIVABLE...
"SOMETHING MORE RUDIMENTARY... LIKE MUSICAL PIPING."
TEKELI-LI!!
TEKELI-LI!!

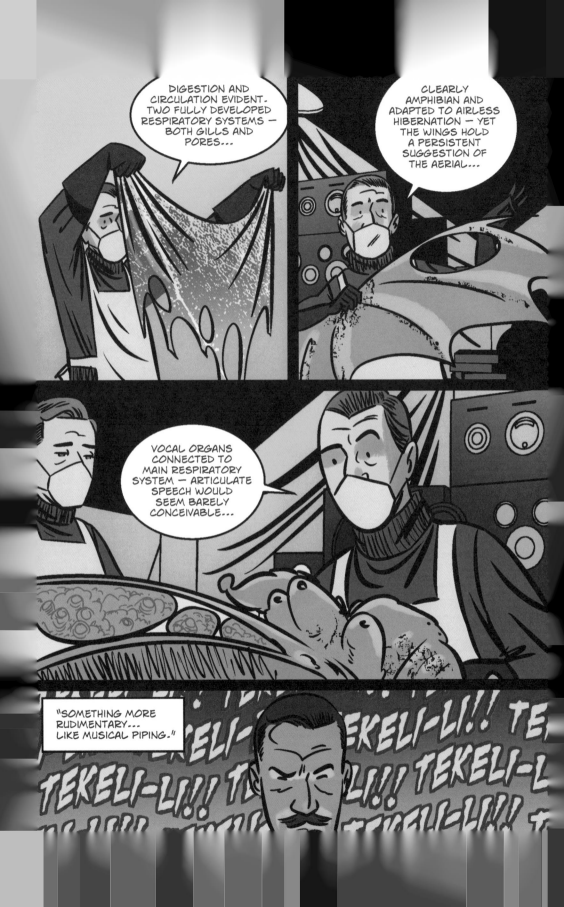

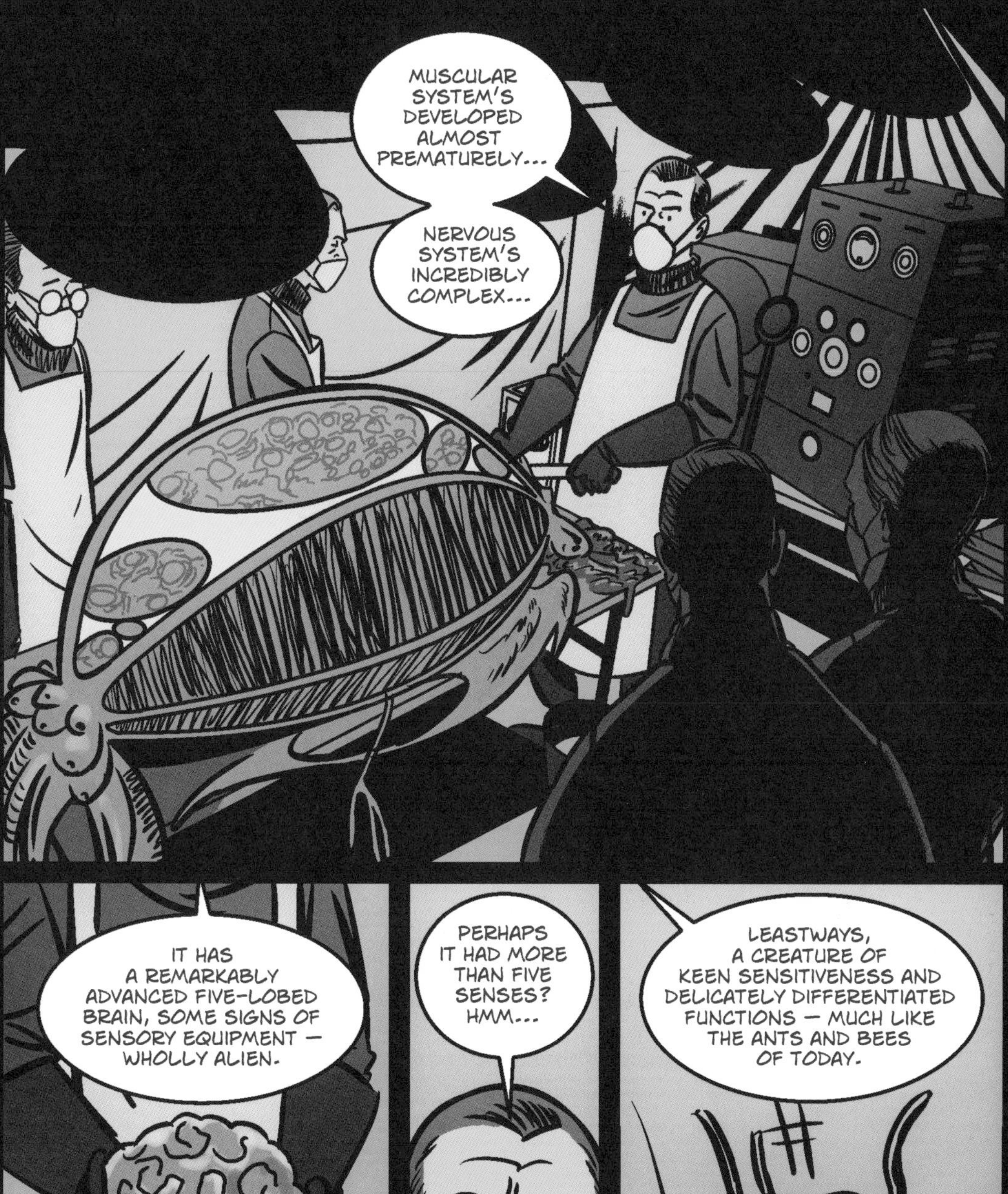
MUSCULAR SYSTEM'S DEVELOPED ALMOST PREMATURELY...
NERVOUS SYSTEM'S INCREDIBLY COMPLEX...
IT HAS A REMARKABLY ADVANCED FIVE-LOBED BRAIN, SOME SIGNS OF SENSORY EQUIPMENT — WHOLLY ALIEN.
PERHAPS IT HAD MORE THAN FIVE SENSES? HMM...
LEASTWAYS, A CREATURE OF KEEN SENSITIVENESS AND DELICATELY DIFFERENTIATED FUNCTIONS — MUCH LIKE THE ANTS AND BEES OF TODAY.
SLOP!

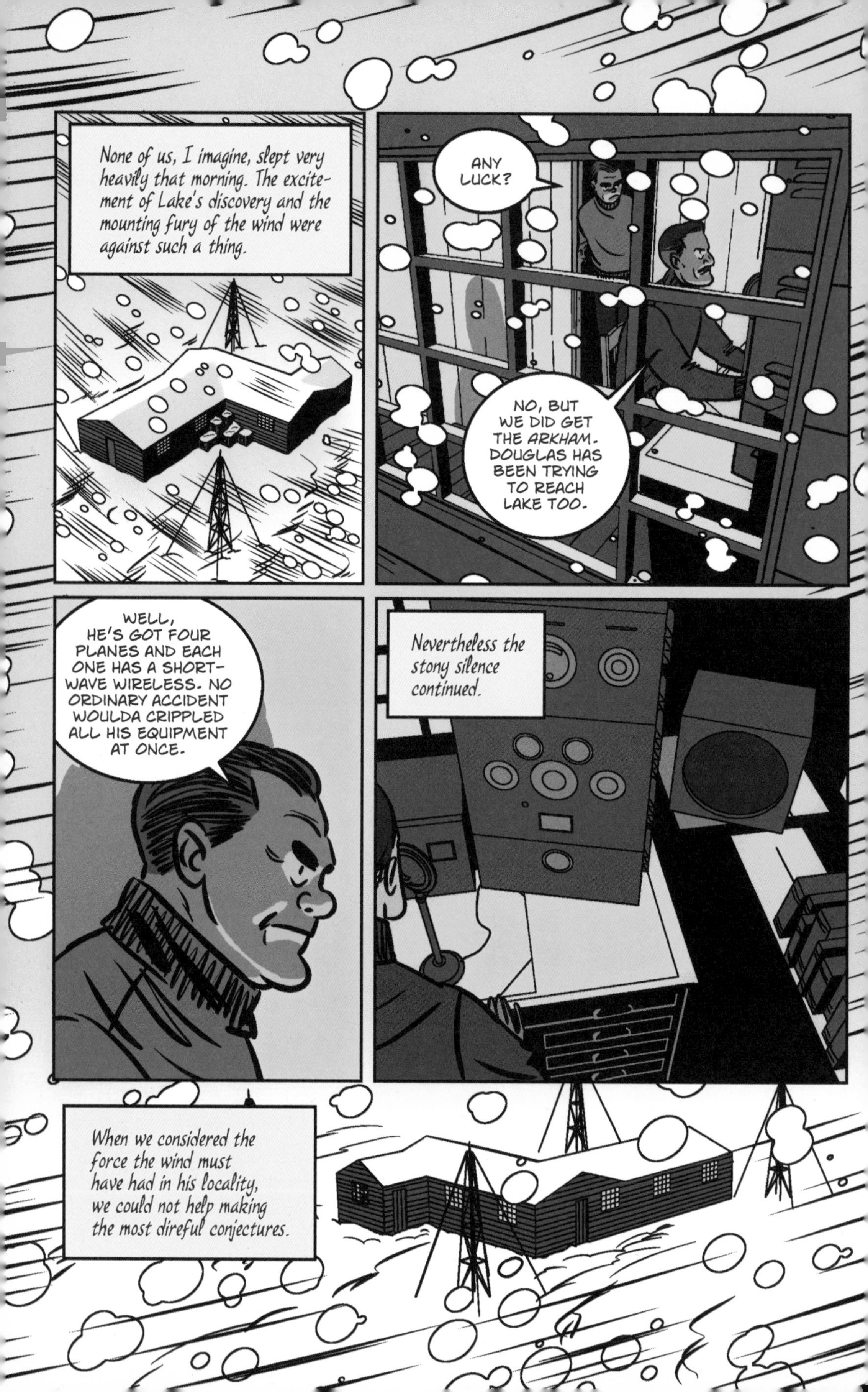
None of us, I imagine, slept very heavily that morning. The excitement of Lake's discovery and the mounting fury of the wind were against such a thing.
ANY LUCK?
NO, BUT WE DID GET THE ARKHAM. DOUGLAS HAS BEEN TRYING TO REACH LAKE TOO.
WELL, HE'S GOT FOUR PLANES AND EACH ONE HAS A SHORT-WAVE WIRELESS. NO ORDINARY ACCIDENT WOULDA CRIPPLED ALL HIS EQUIPMENT AT ONCE.
Nevertheless the stony silence continued.
When we considered the force the wind must have had in his locality, we could not help making the most direful conjectures.

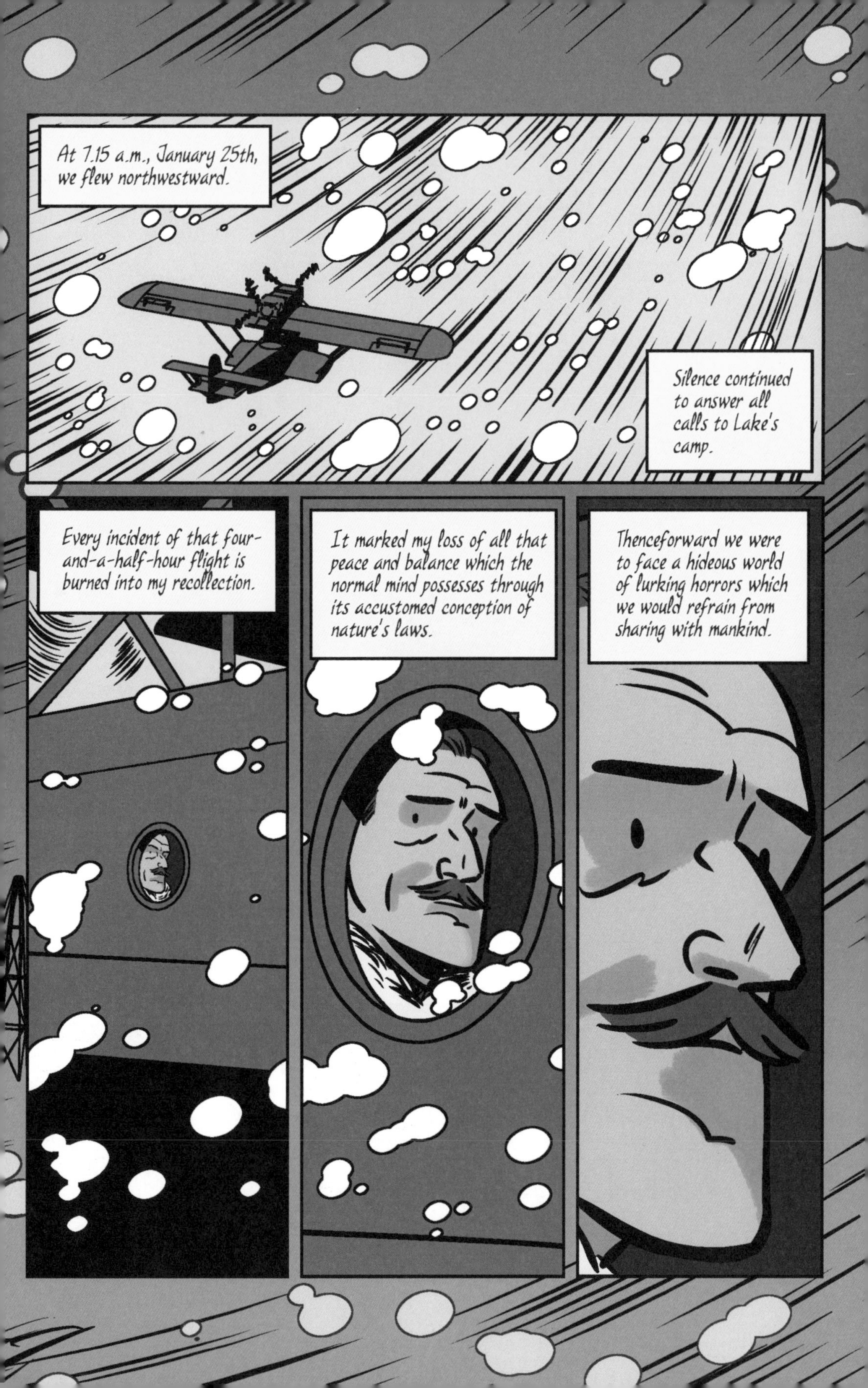
At 7.15 a.m., January 25th, we flew northwestward.
Silence continued to answer all calls to Lake's camp.
Every incident of that four-and-a-half-hour flight is burned into my recollection.
It marked my loss of all that peace and balance which the normal mind possesses through its accustomed conception of nature's laws.
Thenceforward we were to face a hideous world of lurking horrors which we would refrain from sharing with mankind.

At that moment I felt sorry that I had ever read the abhorred Necronomicon.

Some hours after our landing we sent a guarded report of the tragedy we found.

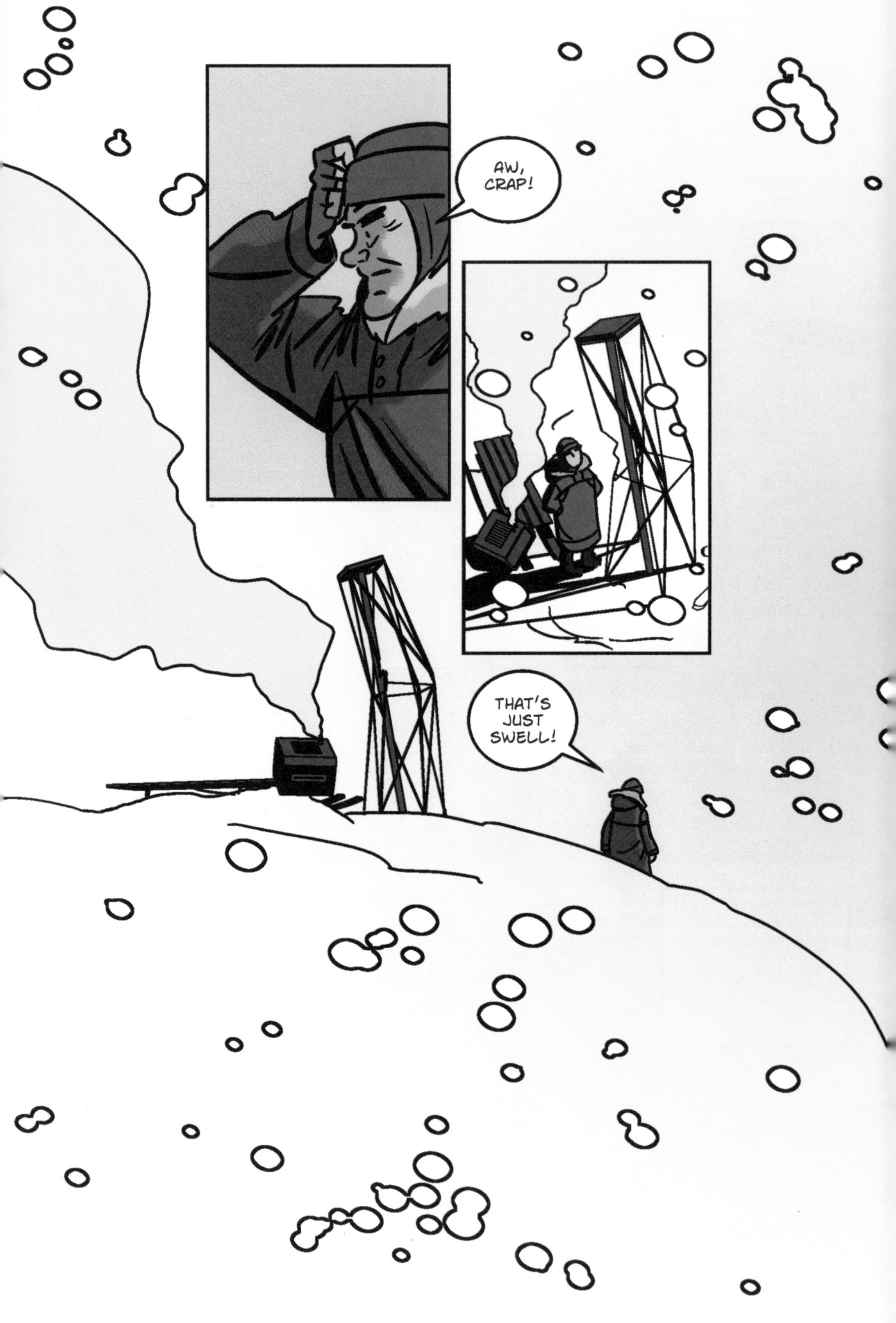
AW, CRAP!
THAT'S JUST SWELL!

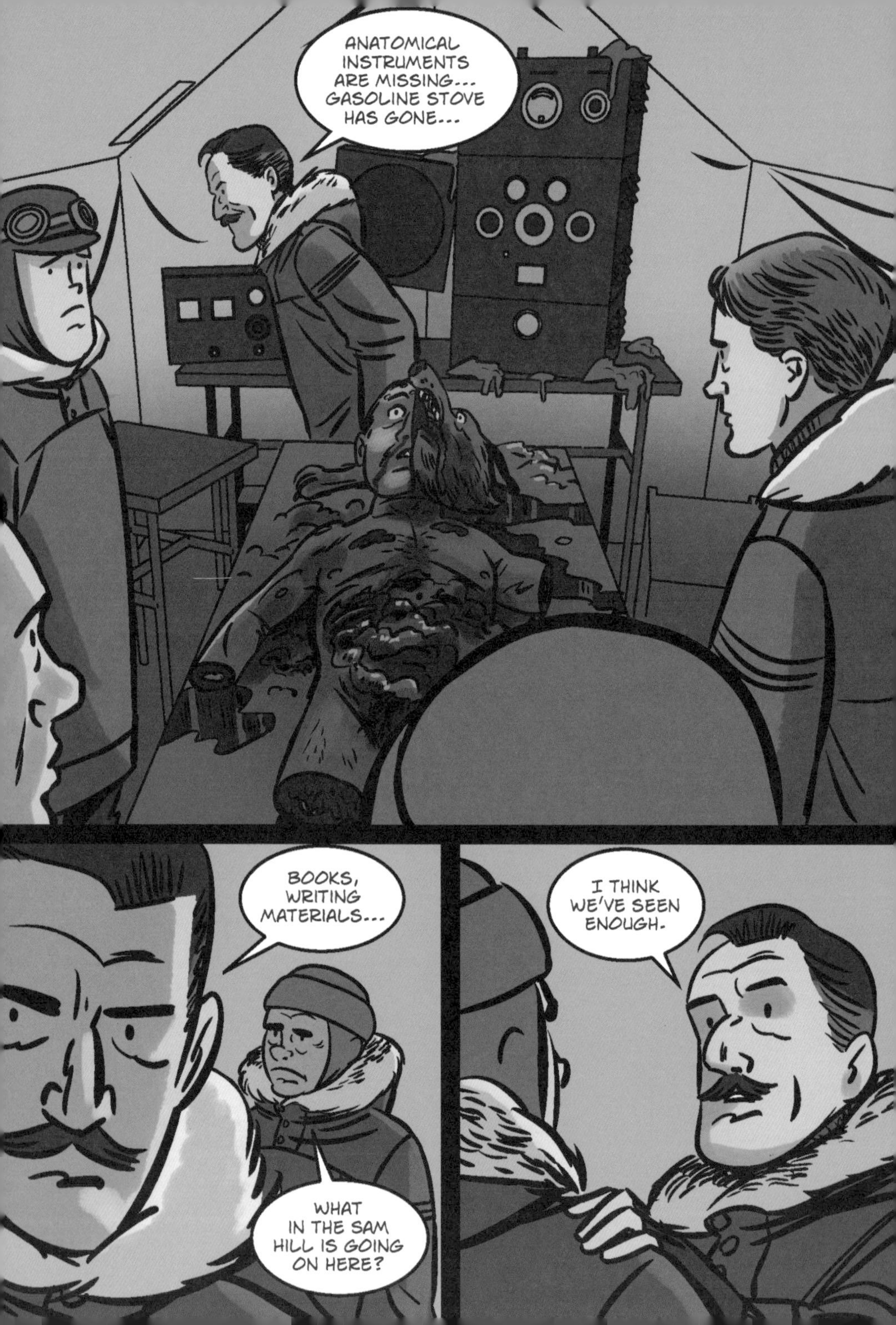
ANATOMICAL INSTRUMENTS ARE MISSING... GASOLINE STOVE HAS GONE...
BOOKS, WRITING MATERIALS...
WHAT IN THE SAM HILL IS GOING ON HERE?
I THINK WE'VE SEEN ENOUGH.

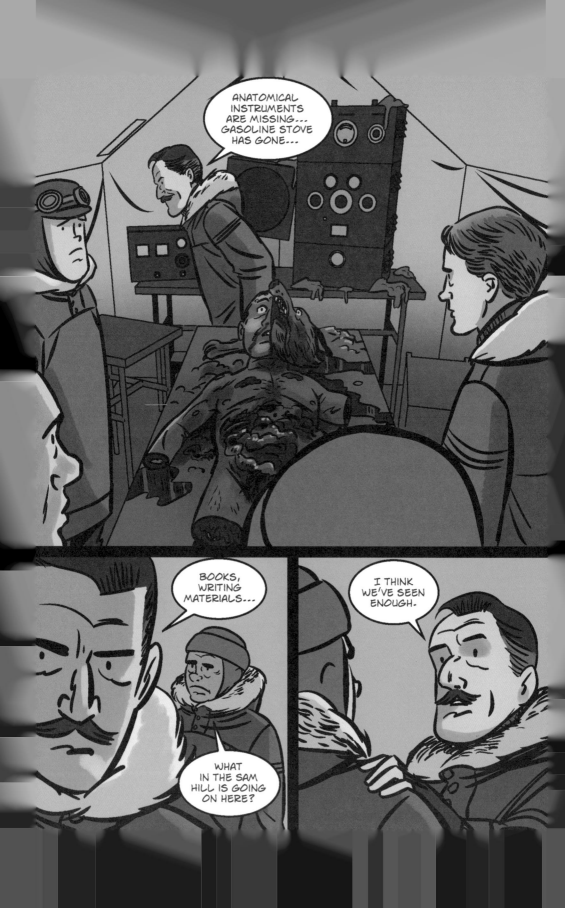

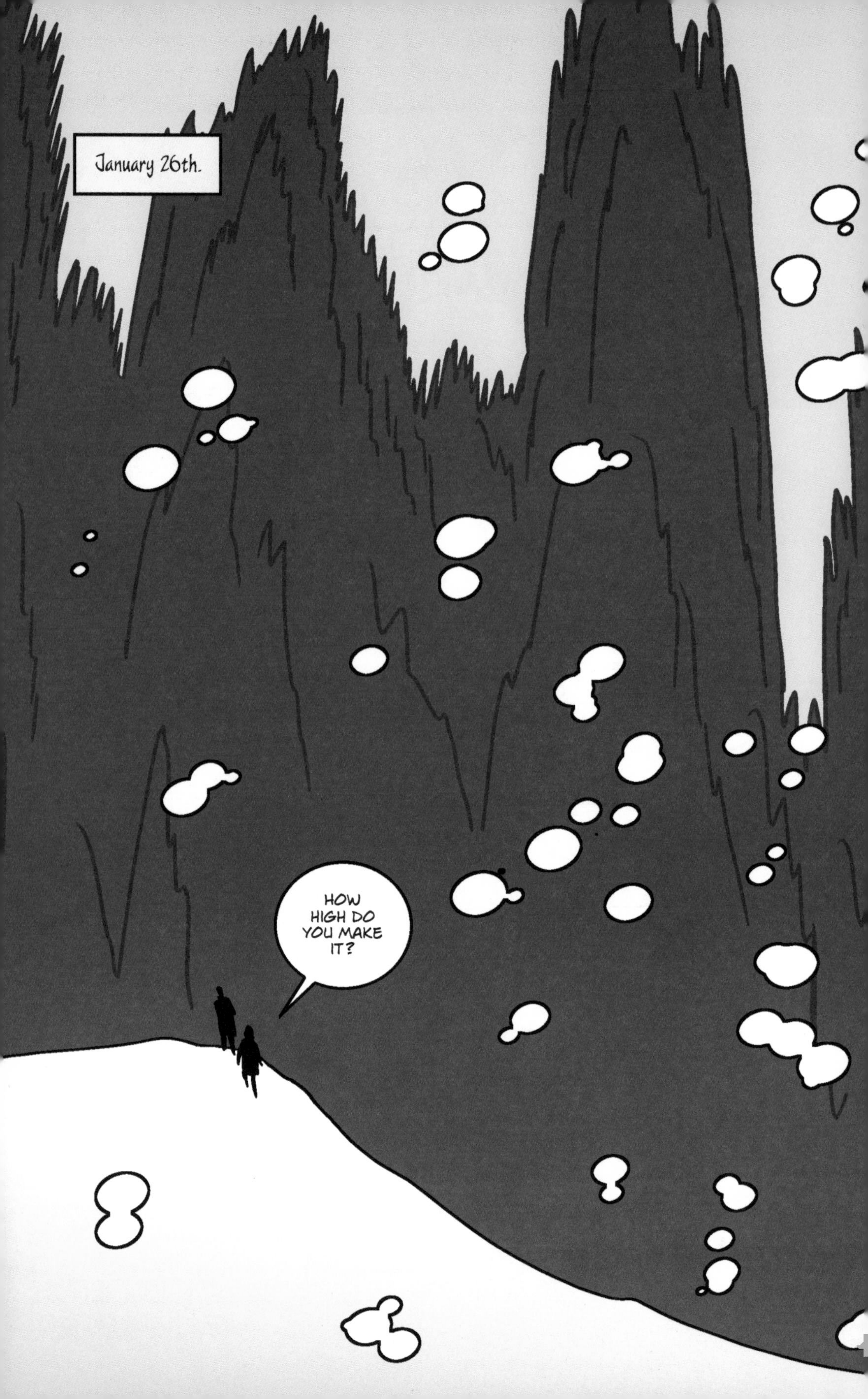
January 26th.
HOW HIGH DO YOU MAKE IT?

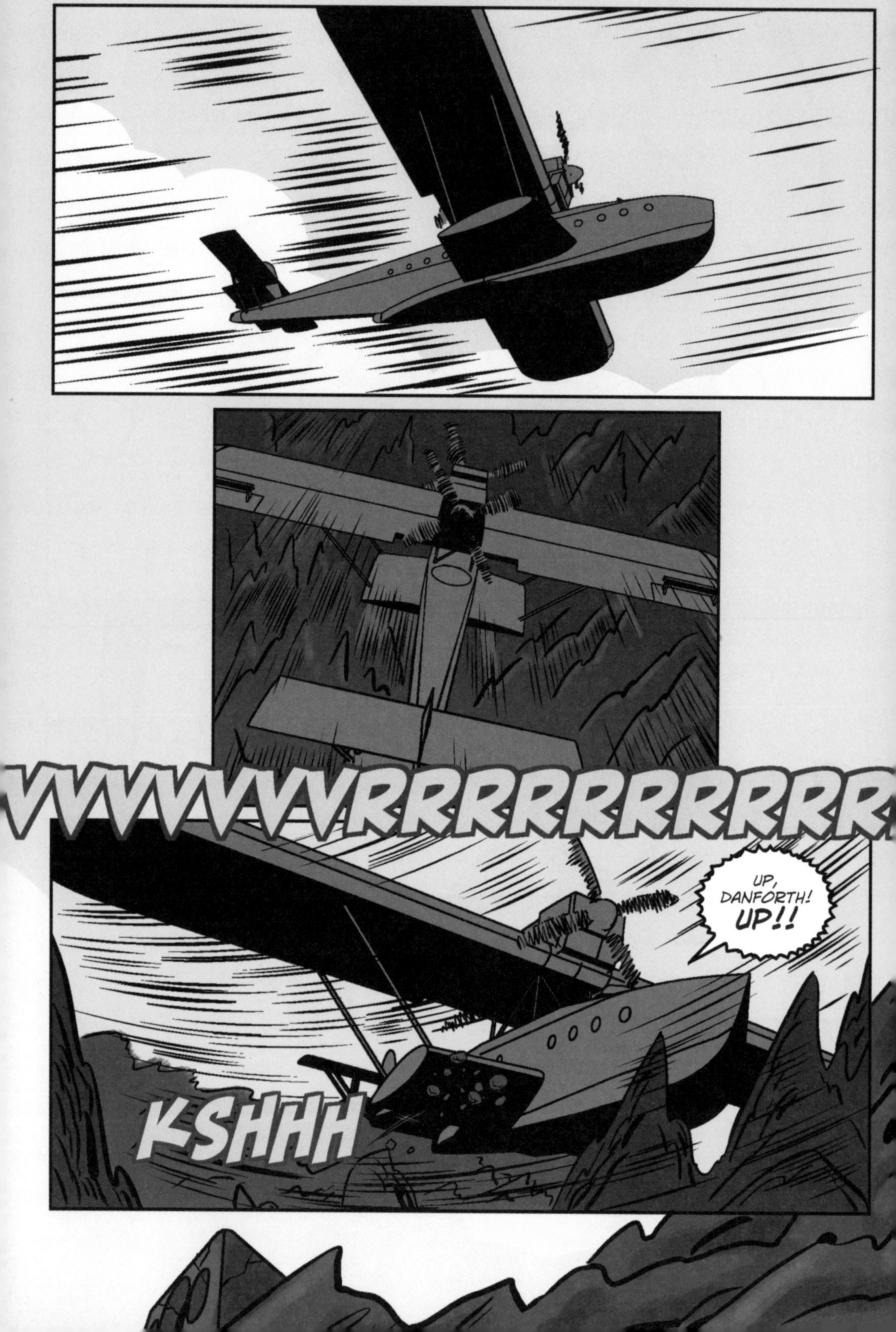
VVVVVVVRRRRRRRRRRR
UP, DANFORTH! UP!!
KSHHH

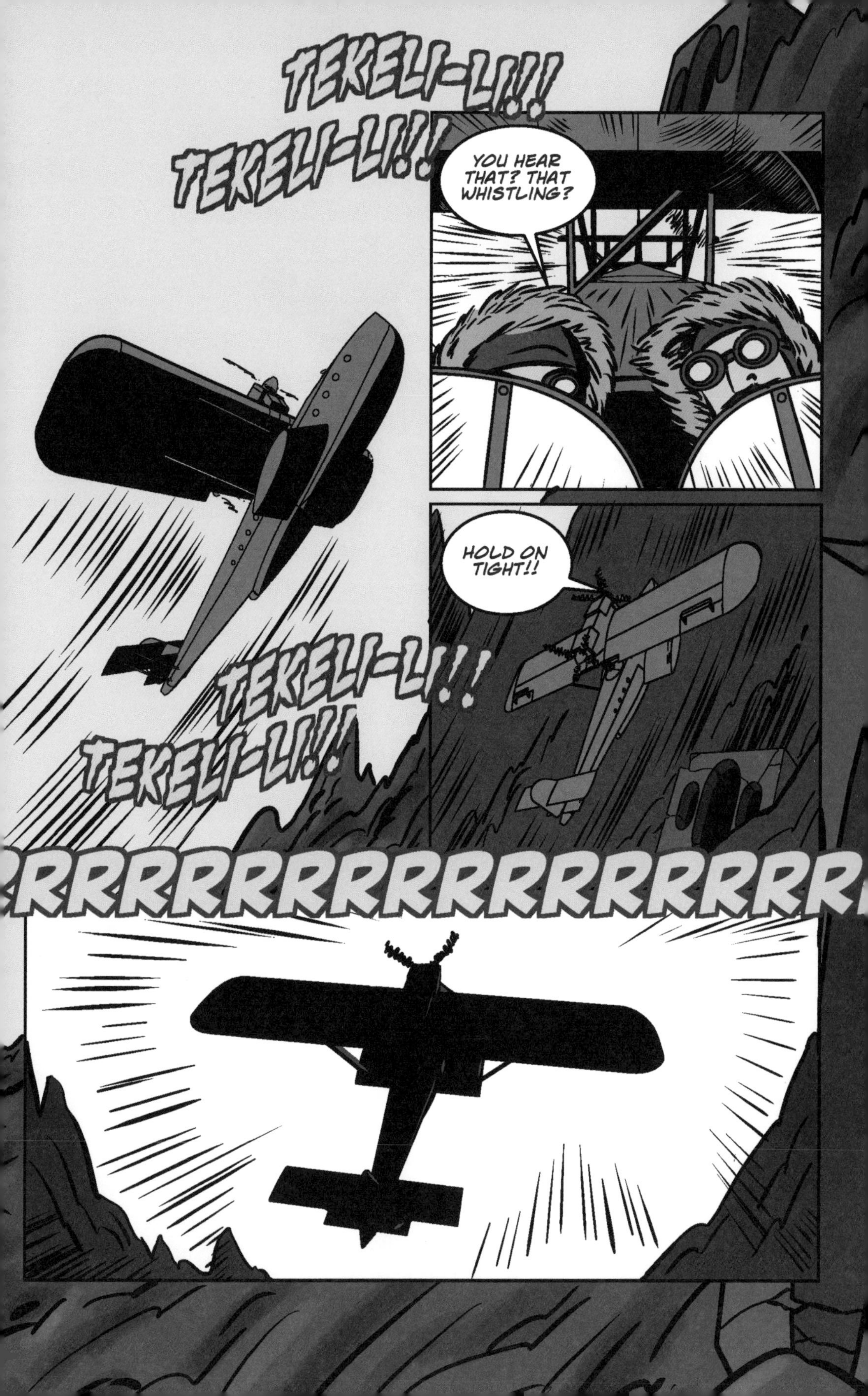
TEKELI-LI!!
TEKELI-LI!!
YOU HEAR THAT? THAT WHISTLING?
HOLD ON TIGHT!!
TEKELI-LI!!
TEKELI-LI!!
RRRRRRRRRRRRRRRRRR

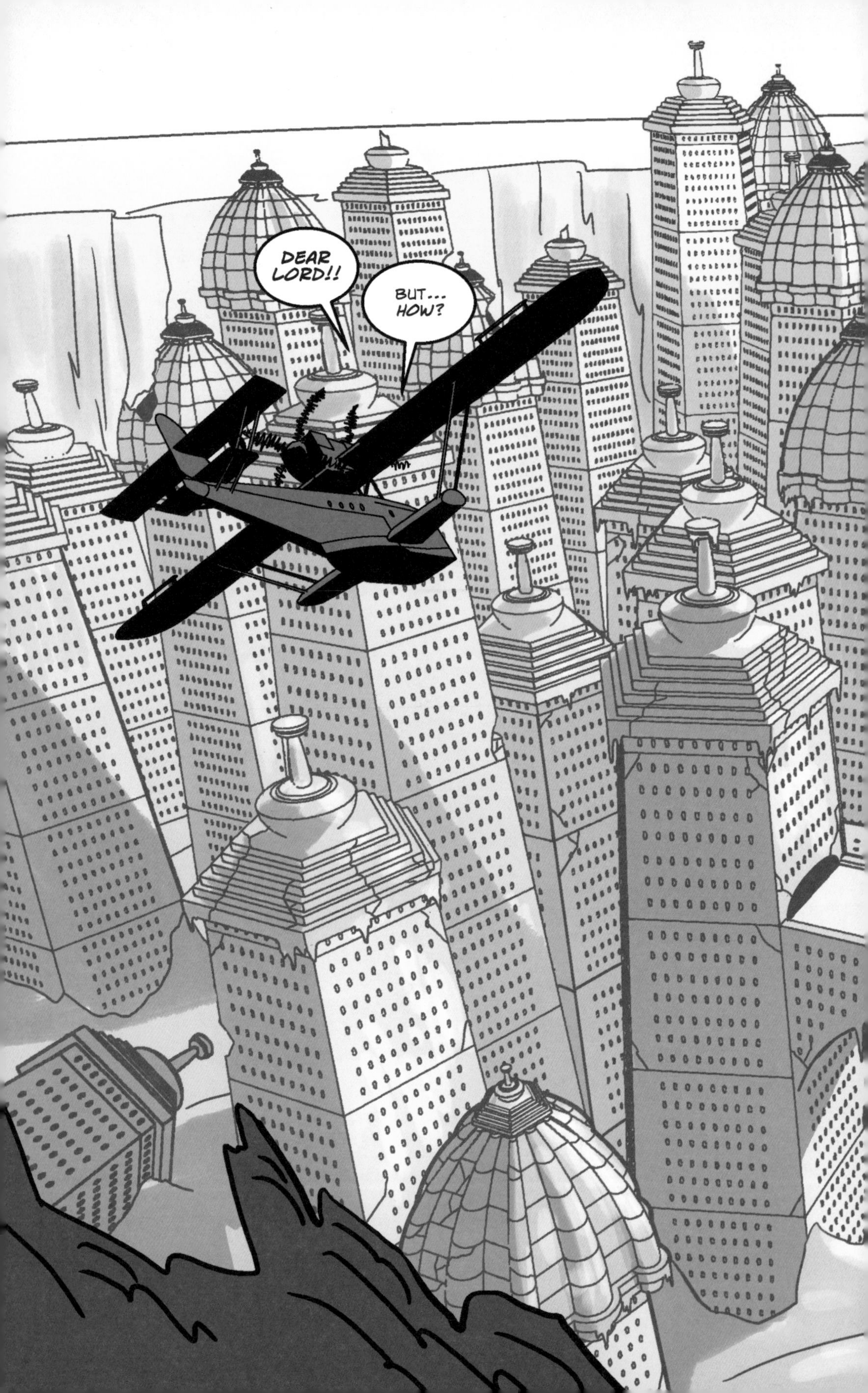
DEAR LORD!!
BUT... HOW?

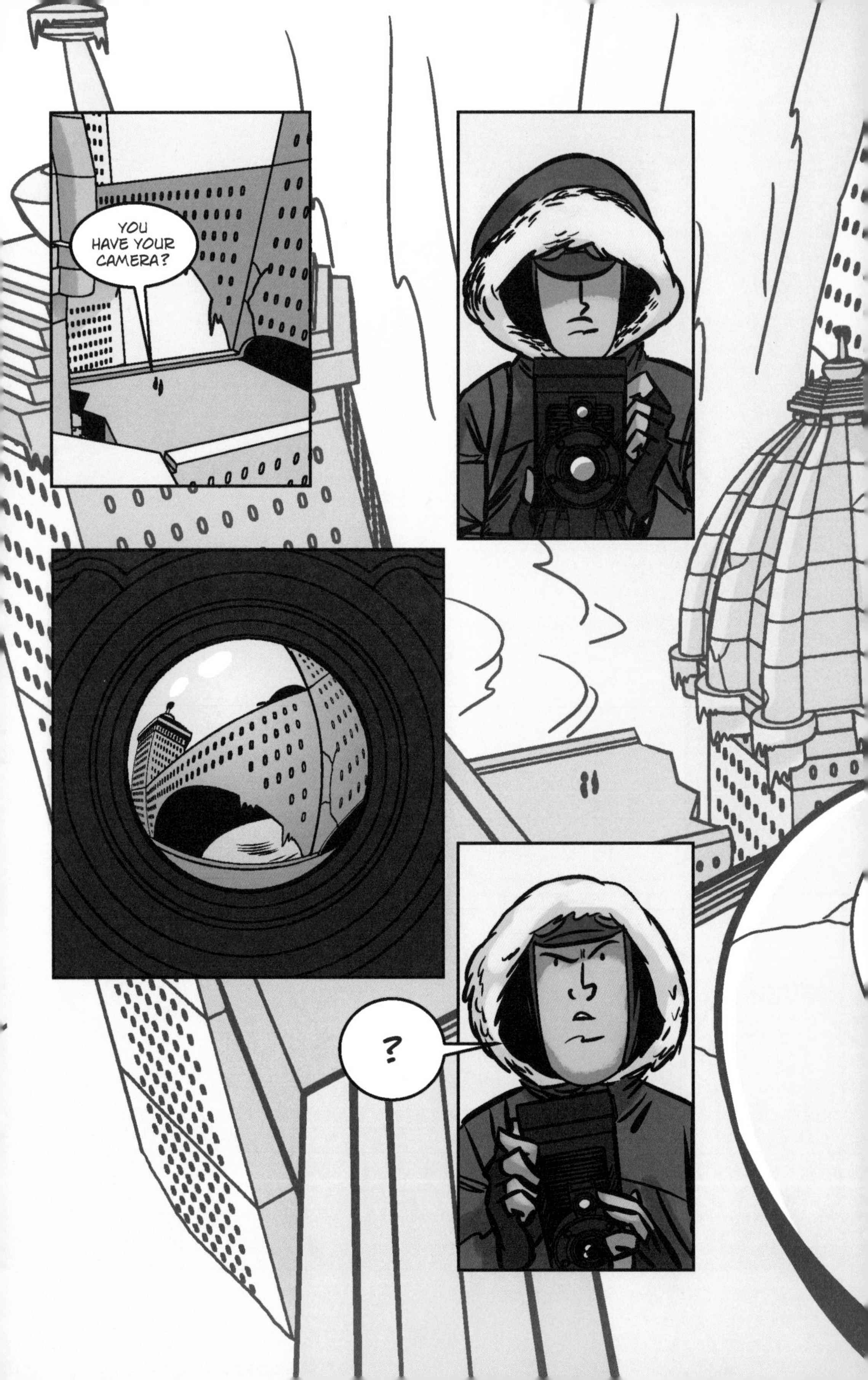
YOU HAVE YOUR CAMERA?
?

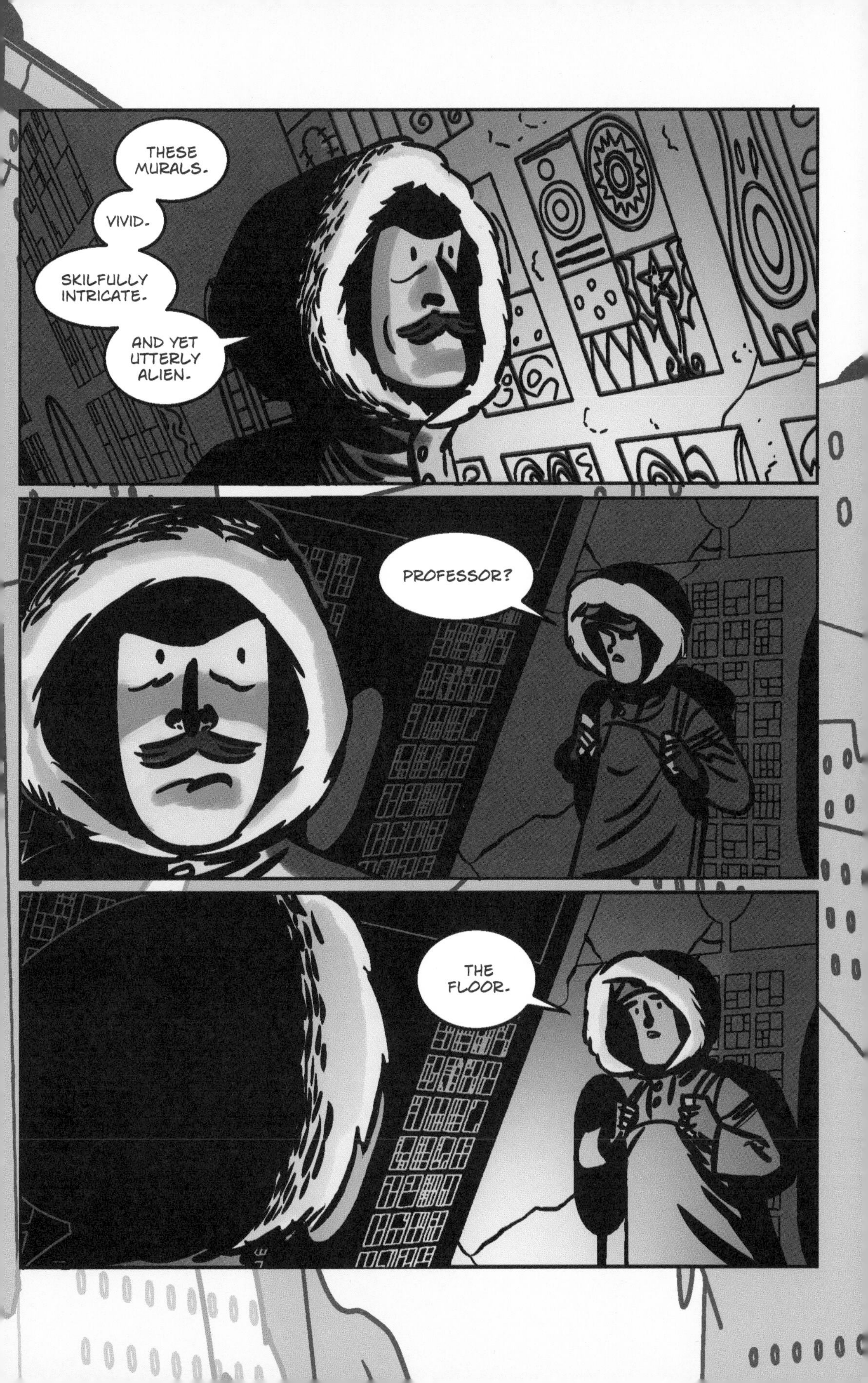
THESE MURALS.
VIVID.
SKILFULLY INTRICATE.
AND YET UTTERLY ALIEN.
PROFESSOR?
THE FLOOR.

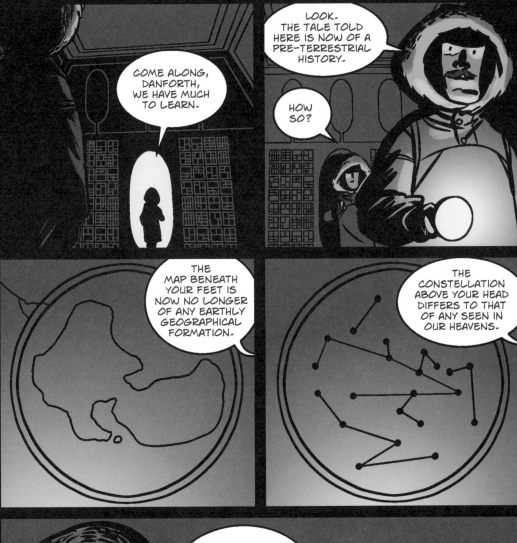

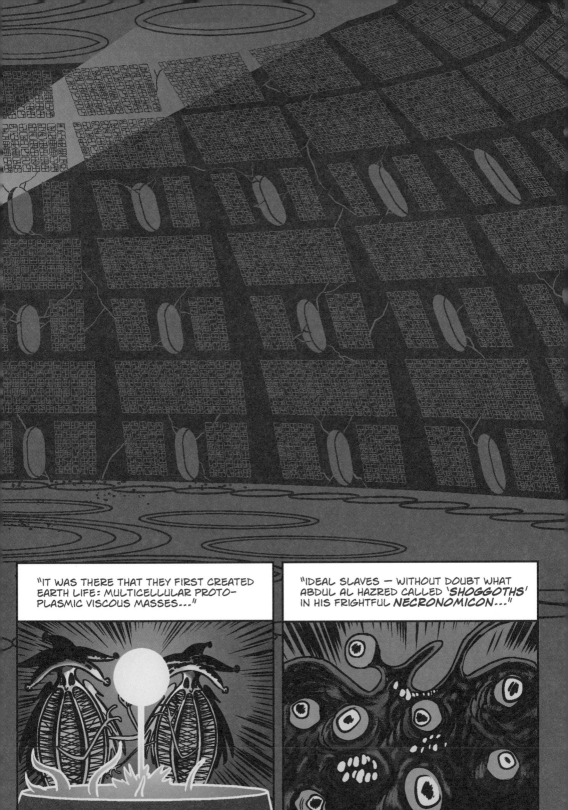

"IT WAS THERE THAT THEY FIRST CREATED EARTH LIFE: MULTICELLULAR PROTO-PLASMIC VISCOUS MASSES..."

"IDEAL SLAVES — WITHOUT DOUBT WHAT ABDUL AL HAZRED CALLED 'SHOGGOTHS' IN HIS FRIGHTFUL *NECRONOMICON*..."

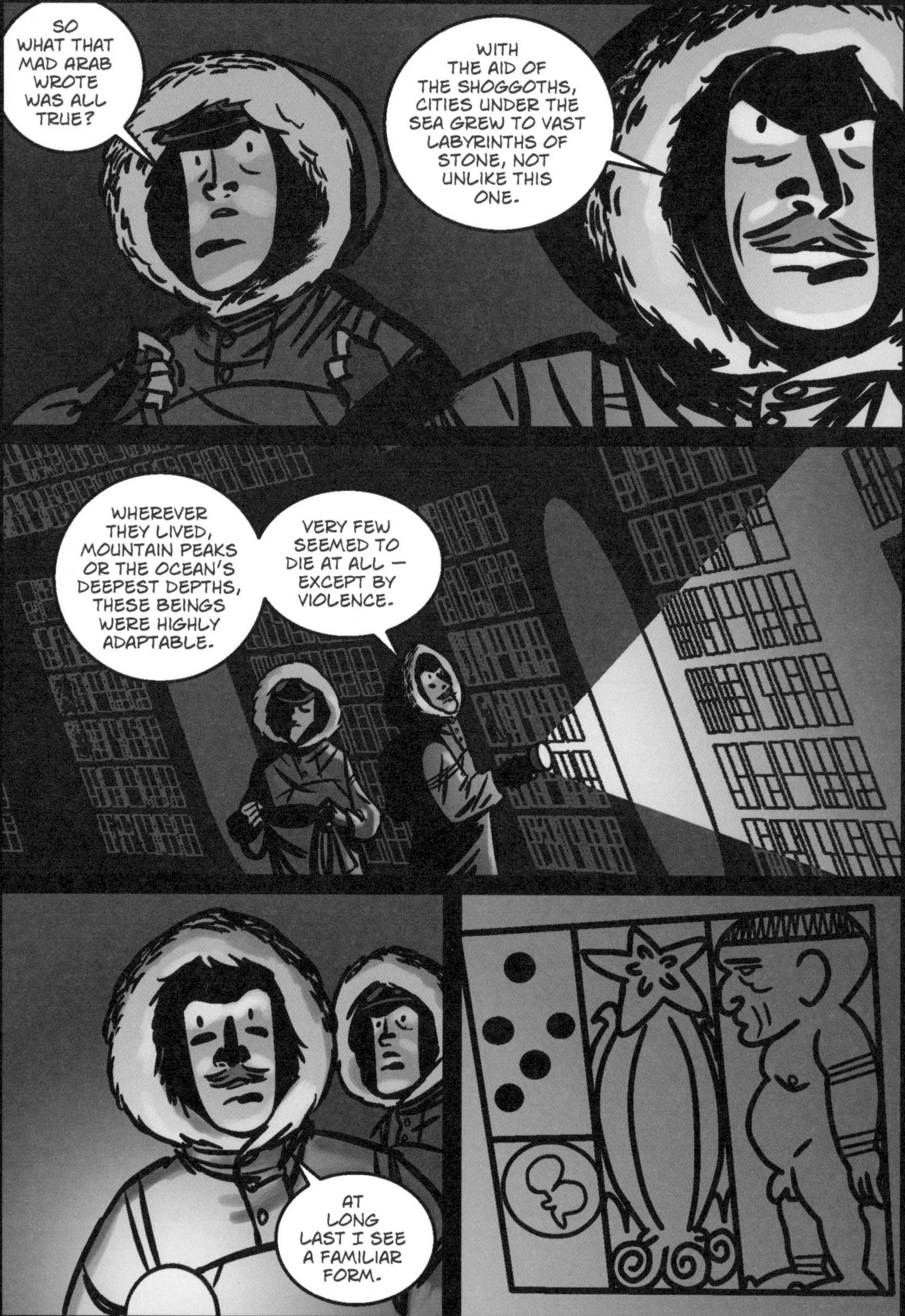
SO WHAT THAT MAD ARAB WROTE WAS ALL TRUE?
WITH THE AID OF THE SHOGGOTHS, CITIES UNDER THE SEA GREW TO VAST LABYRINTHS OF STONE, NOT UNLIKE THIS ONE.
WHEREVER THEY LIVED, MOUNTAIN PEAKS OR THE OCEAN'S DEEPEST DEPTHS, THESE BEINGS WERE HIGHLY ADAPTABLE.
VERY FEW SEEMED TO DIE AT ALL — EXCEPT BY VIOLENCE.
AT LONG LAST I SEE A FAMILIAR FORM.

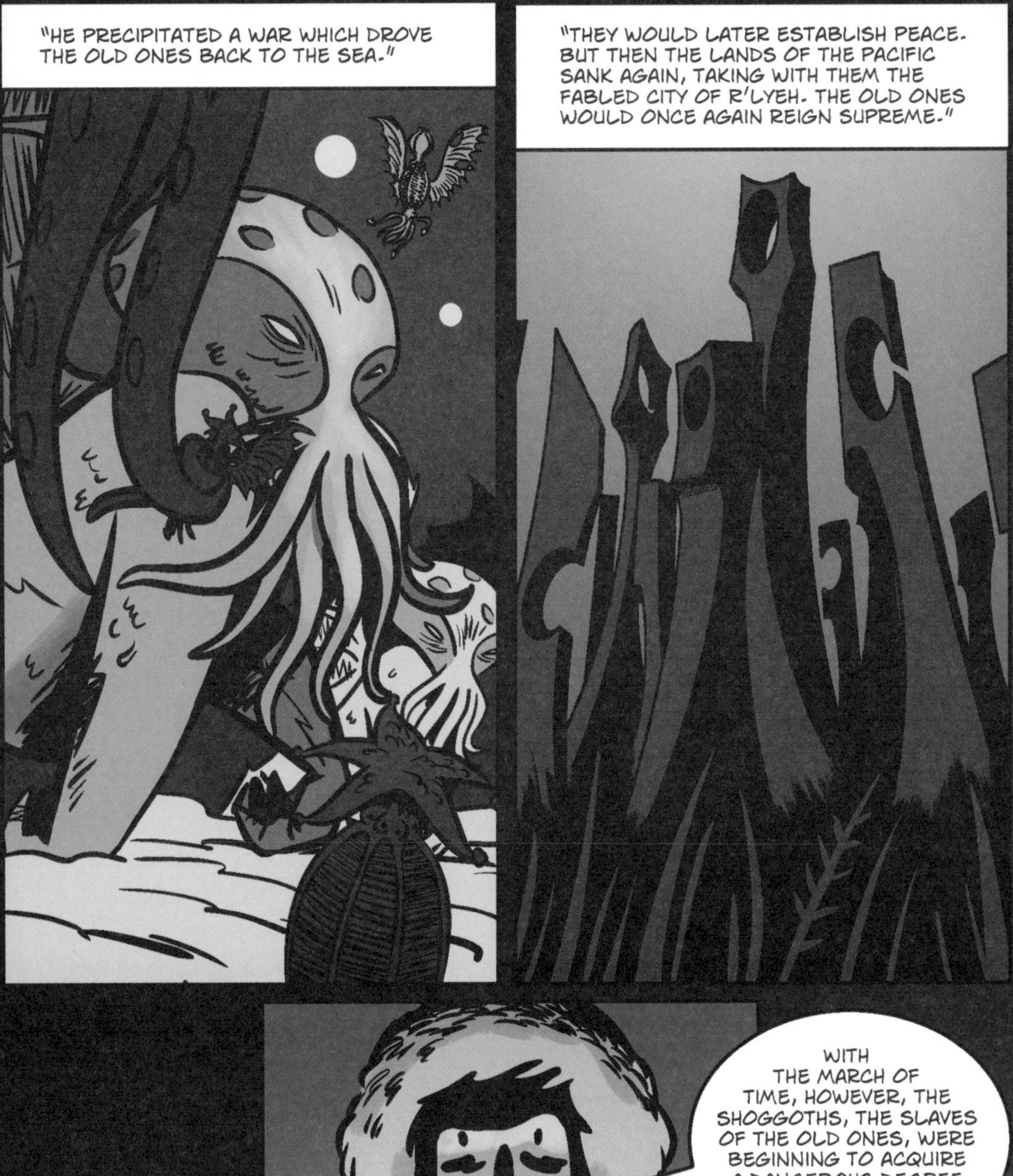
"HE PRECIPITATED A WAR WHICH DROVE THE OLD ONES BACK TO THE SEA."
"THEY WOULD LATER ESTABLISH PEACE. BUT THEN THE LANDS OF THE PACIFIC SANK AGAIN, TAKING WITH THEM THE FABLED CITY OF R'LYEH. THE OLD ONES WOULD ONCE AGAIN REIGN SUPREME."
WITH THE MARCH OF TIME, HOWEVER, THE SHOGGOTHS, THE SLAVES OF THE OLD ONES, WERE BEGINNING TO ACQUIRE A DANGEROUS DEGREE OF ACCIDENTAL INTELLIGENCE.

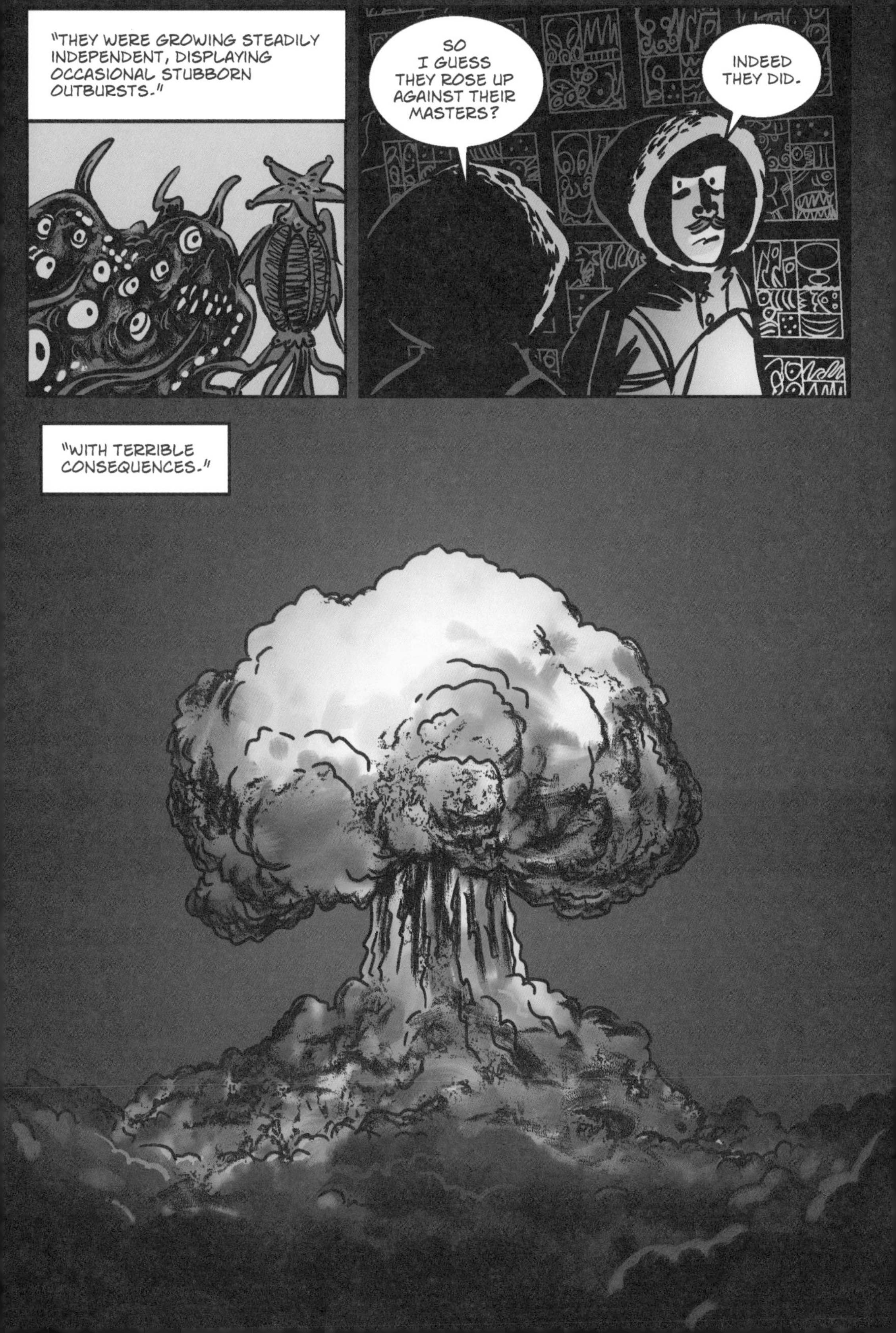
"THEY WERE GROWING STEADILY INDEPENDENT, DISPLAYING OCCASIONAL STUBBORN OUTBURSTS."
SO I GUESS THEY ROSE UP AGAINST THEIR MASTERS?
INDEED THEY DID.
"WITH TERRIBLE CONSEQUENCES."

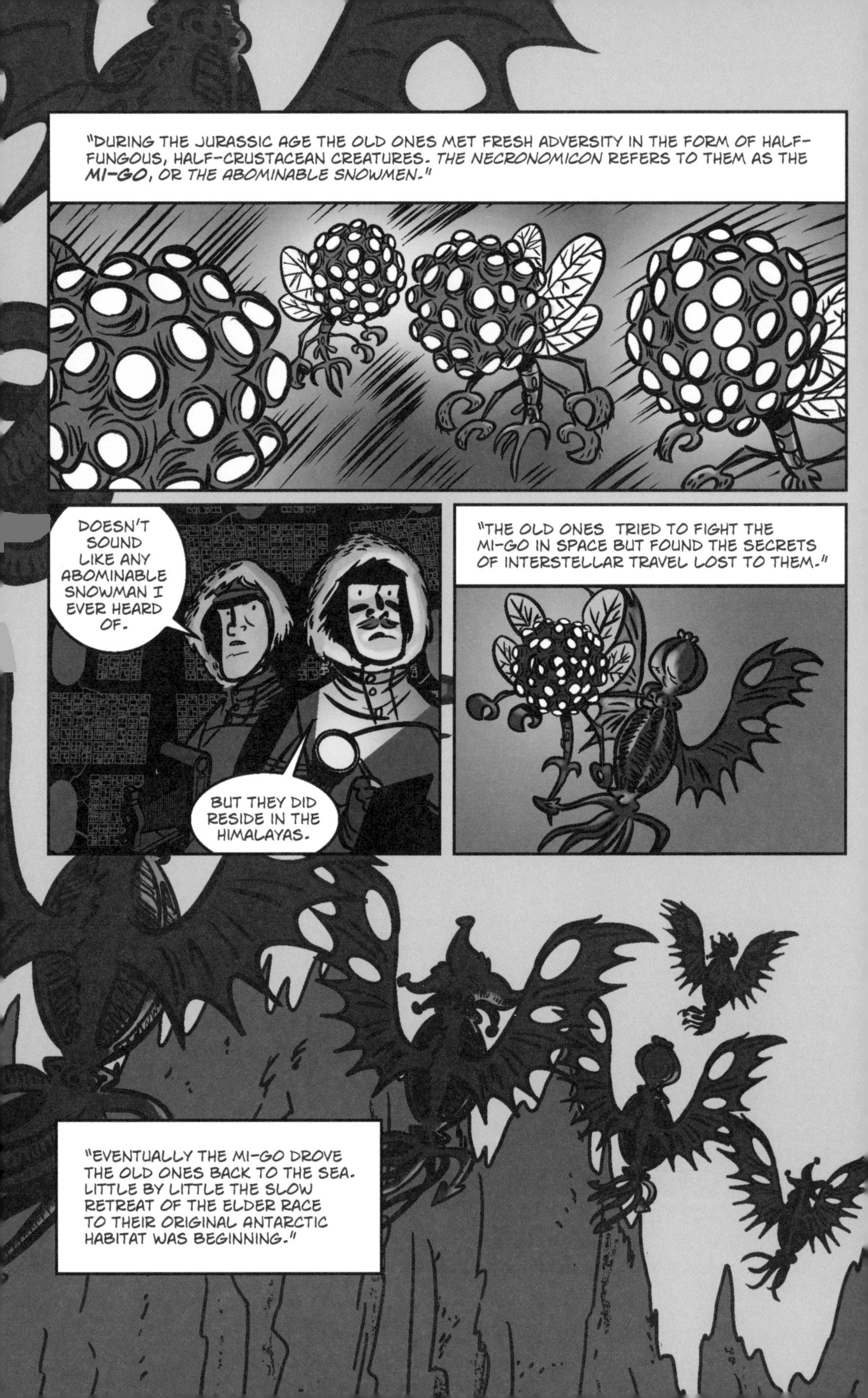
"DURING THE JURASSIC AGE THE OLD ONES MET FRESH ADVERSITY IN THE FORM OF HALF-FUNGOUS, HALF-CRUSTACEAN CREATURES. *THE NECRONOMICON* REFERS TO THEM AS THE ***MI-GO***, OR *THE ABOMINABLE SNOWMEN*."
DOESN'T SOUND LIKE ANY ABOMINABLE SNOWMAN I EVER HEARD OF.
BUT THEY DID RESIDE IN THE HIMALAYAS.
"THE OLD ONES TRIED TO FIGHT THE MI-GO IN SPACE BUT FOUND THE SECRETS OF INTERSTELLAR TRAVEL LOST TO THEM."
"EVENTUALLY THE MI-GO DROVE THE OLD ONES BACK TO THE SEA. LITTLE BY LITTLE THE SLOW RETREAT OF THE ELDER RACE TO THEIR ORIGINAL ANTARCTIC HABITAT WAS BEGINNING."

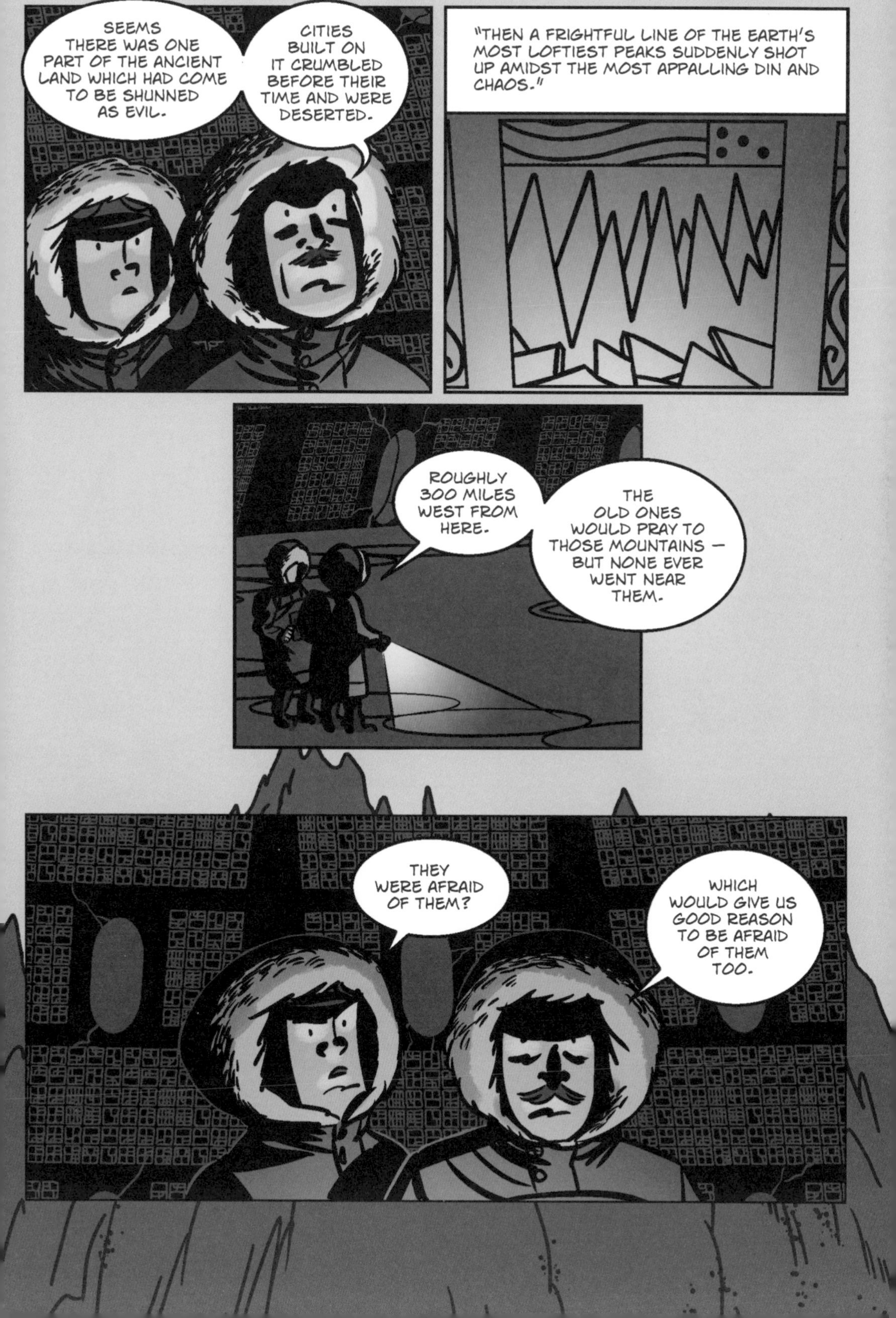
SEEMS THERE WAS ONE PART OF THE ANCIENT LAND WHICH HAD COME TO BE SHUNNED AS EVIL.
CITIES BUILT ON IT CRUMBLED BEFORE THEIR TIME AND WERE DESERTED.
"THEN A FRIGHTFUL LINE OF THE EARTH'S MOST LOFTIEST PEAKS SUDDENLY SHOT UP AMIDST THE MOST APPALLING DIN AND CHAOS."
ROUGHLY 300 MILES WEST FROM HERE.
THE OLD ONES WOULD PRAY TO THOSE MOUNTAINS — BUT NONE EVER WENT NEAR THEM.
THEY WERE AFRAID OF THEM?
WHICH WOULD GIVE US GOOD REASON TO BE AFRAID OF THEM TOO.

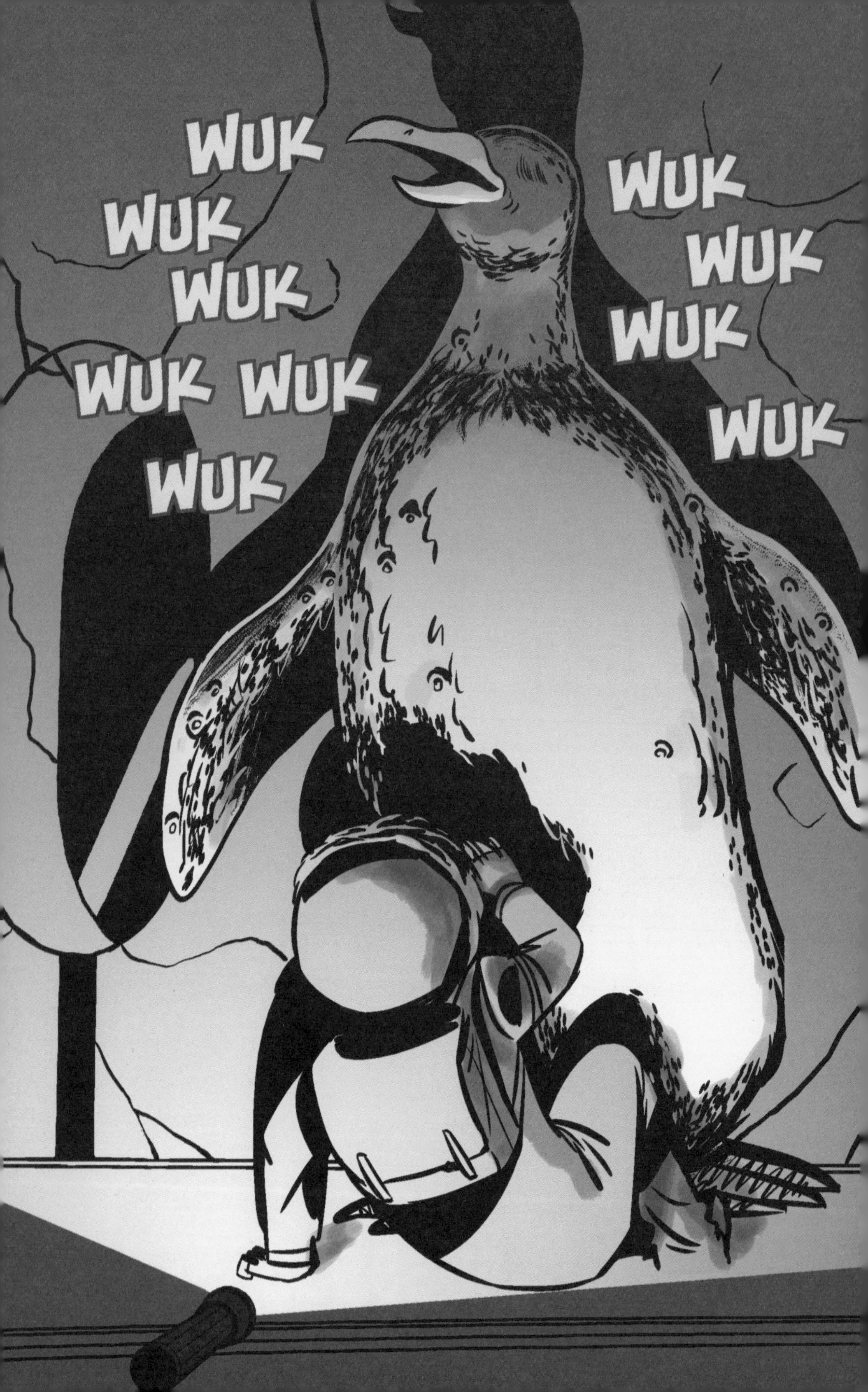
WUK
WUK
WUK
WUK WUK
WUK
WUK
WUK
WUK
WUK

CARE-FULLY NOW.
THEIR EYES! WHERE ARE THEIR EYES?
HHHHHSSSSS
WHAT NEED HAVE THEY FOR EYES IN THE PERPETUAL DARKNESS OF A SUNLESS SEA?
HHHHHSSSSS
WHERE DO YOU THINK IT'S GOING?
LET'S FIND OUT, SHALL WE?
SO LONG AS WE DON'T MAKE TOO MUCH NOISE WE SHOULDN'T GET ANY TROUBLE FROM OUR SIGHTLESS FRIEND.
WUK WUK WUK WUK WUK

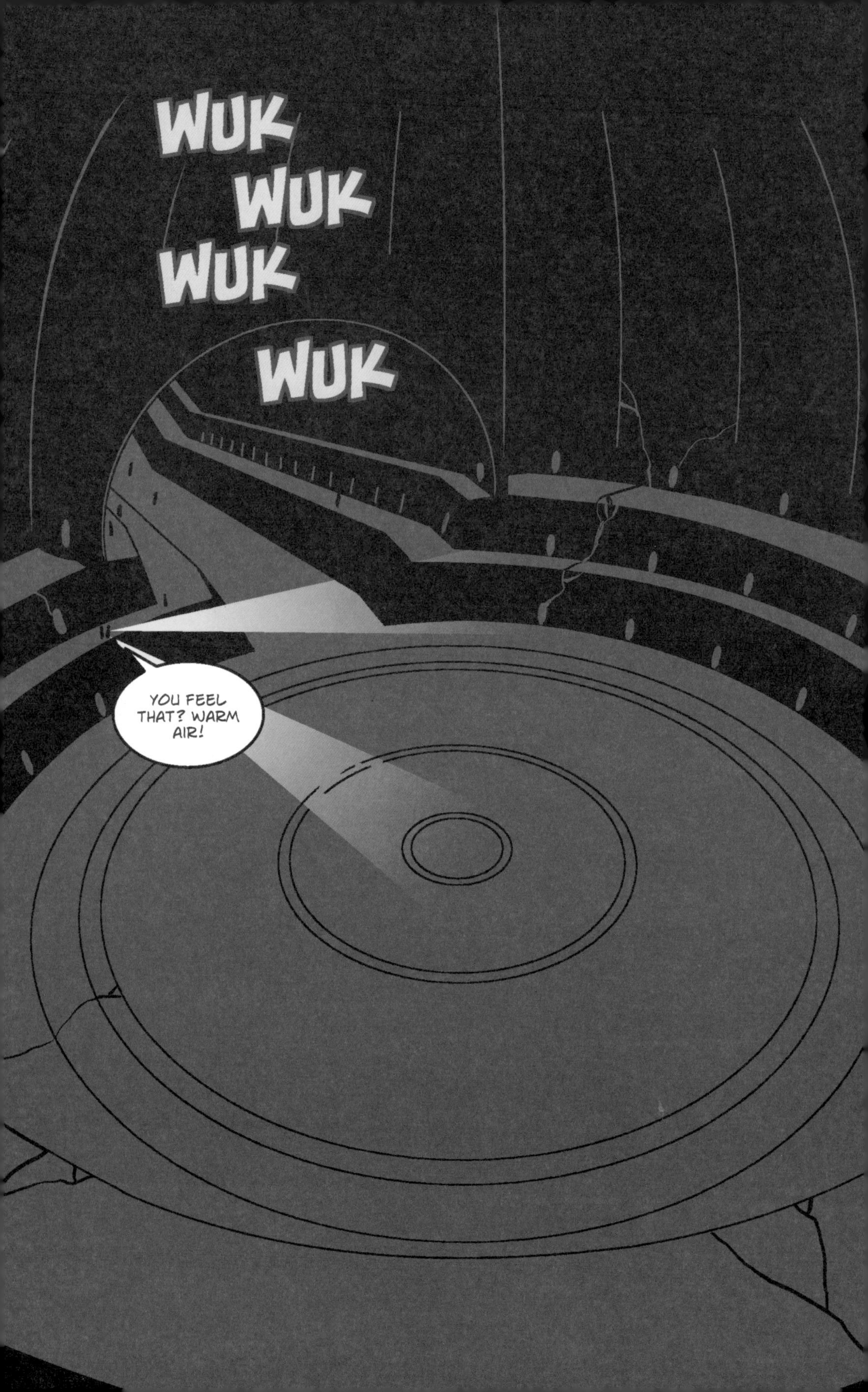
WUK
WUK
WUK
WUK
YOU FEEL THAT? WARM AIR!

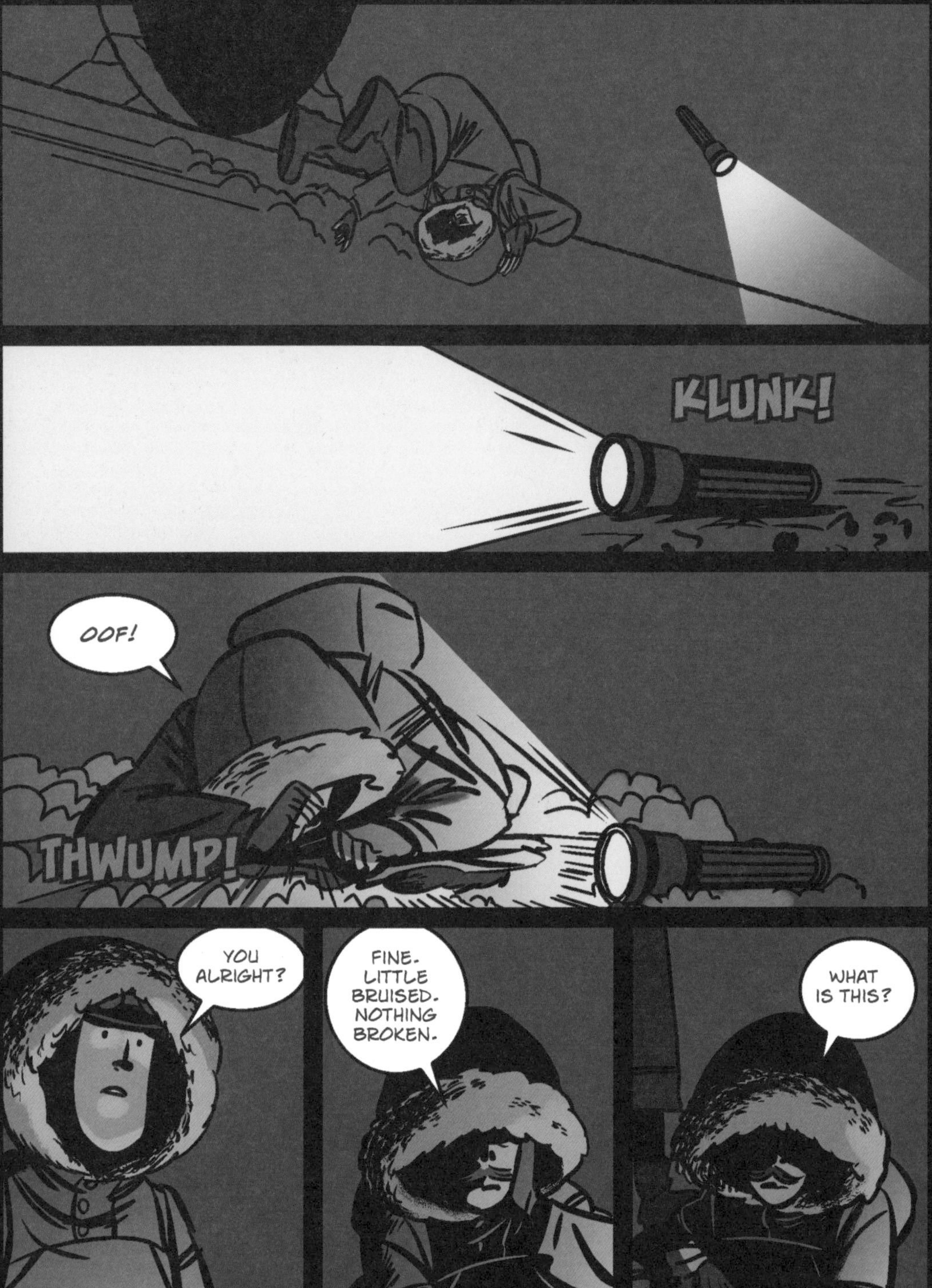
KLUNK!
OOF!
THWUMP!
YOU ALRIGHT?
FINE. LITTLE BRUISED. NOTHING BROKEN.
WHAT IS THIS?

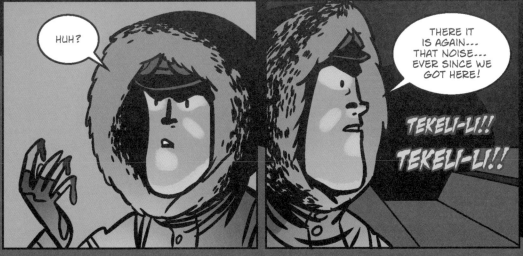

ONLY NOW... NOW IT SOUNDS LIKE... LIKE A TRAIN...
TEKELI-LI!! TEKELI-LI!!
TEKELI-LI!! TEKELI-LI!!
TEKELI-LI!! TEKELI-LI!!
TEKELI-LI!! TEKELI-LI!!
DANFORTH?
TEKELI-LI!!
TEKELI-LI!!
YES, PROFESSOR?
TEKELI-LI!!
TEKELI-LI!!
TEKELI-LI!! TEKELI-LI!!

WUK WUK WUK WUK WUK
TEKELI-LI!!
TEKELI-LI!!
TEKELI-LI!!
TEKELI-LI!!
WUK
WUK
WUK
WUK
RUN!!
TEKELI-LI!!
TEKELI-LI!!
TEKELI-LI!!
TEKELI-LI!!
TEKELI-LI!!
TEKELI-LI!!
WUK
WUK
WUK WUK WUK

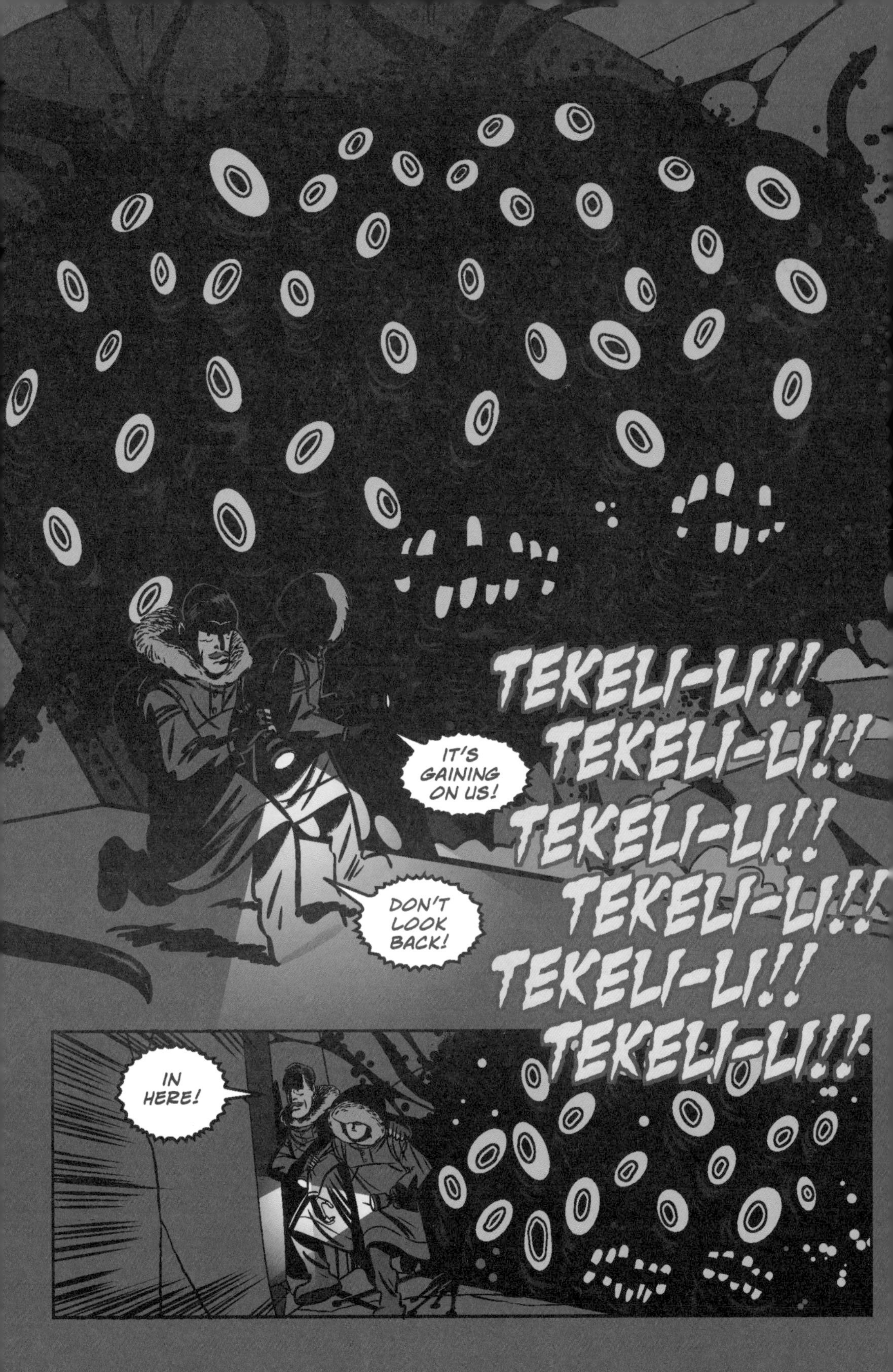
TEKELI-LI!!
TEKELI-LI!!
IT'S GAINING ON US!
TEKELI-LI!!
TEKELI-LI!!
DON'T LOOK BACK!
TEKELI-LI!!
TEKELI-LI!!
IN HERE!

SOUTH STATION UNDER...
TEKELI-LI!! TEKELI-LI!!
WASHINGTON UNDER... PARK STREET UNDER KENDALL...
TEKELI-LI!! TEKELI-LI!!
CENTRAL... HARVARD...
DEAR GOD!
TEKELI-LI!! TEKELI-LI!!

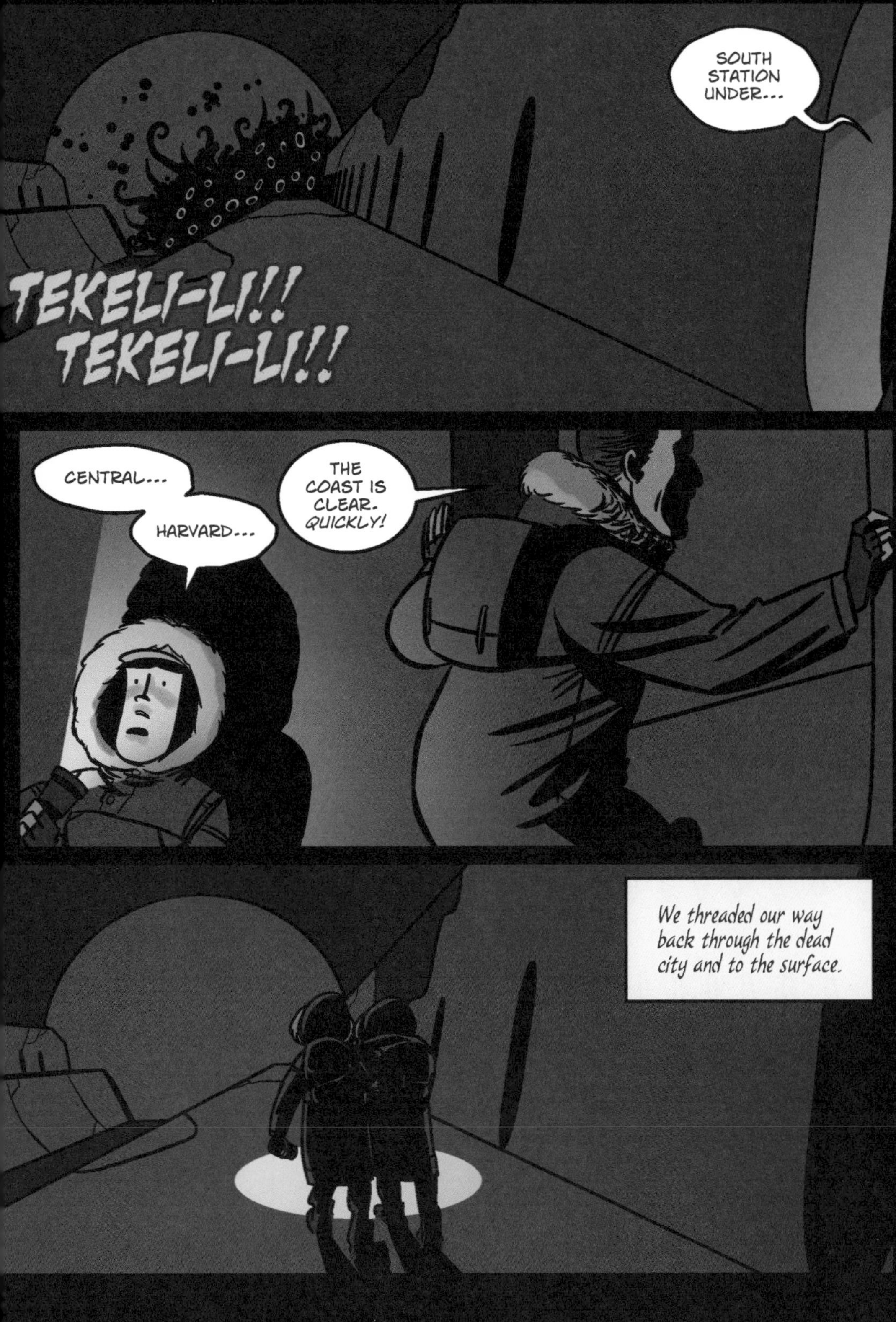
SOUTH STATION UNDER...
TEKELI-LI!! TEKELI-LI!!
CENTRAL...
HARVARD...
THE COAST IS CLEAR. QUICKLY!
We threaded our way back through the dead city and to the surface.

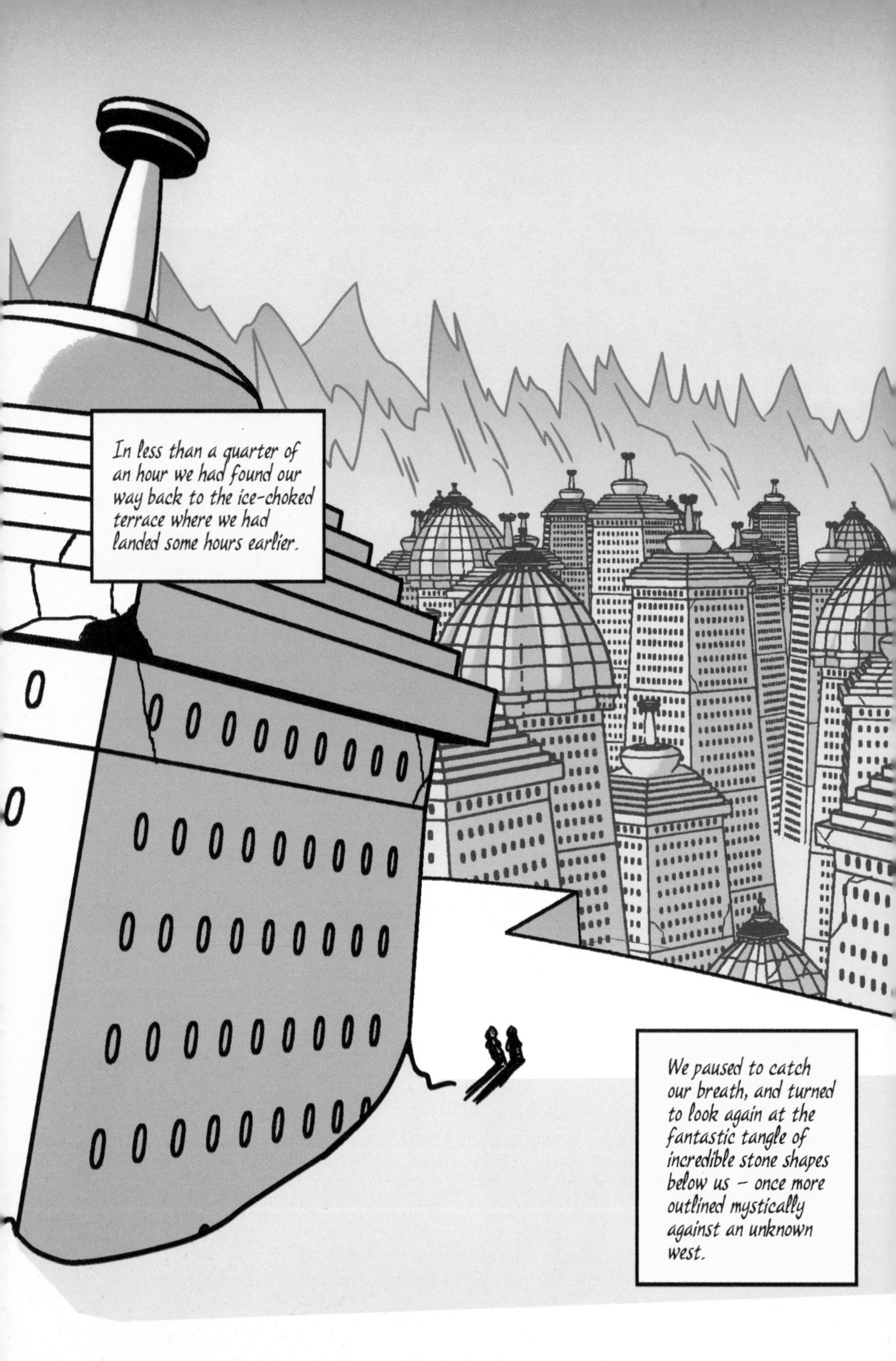
In less than a quarter of an hour we had found our way back to the ice-choked terrace where we had landed some hours earlier.
We paused to catch our breath, and turned to look again at the fantastic tangle of incredible stone shapes below us – once more outlined mystically against an unknown west.

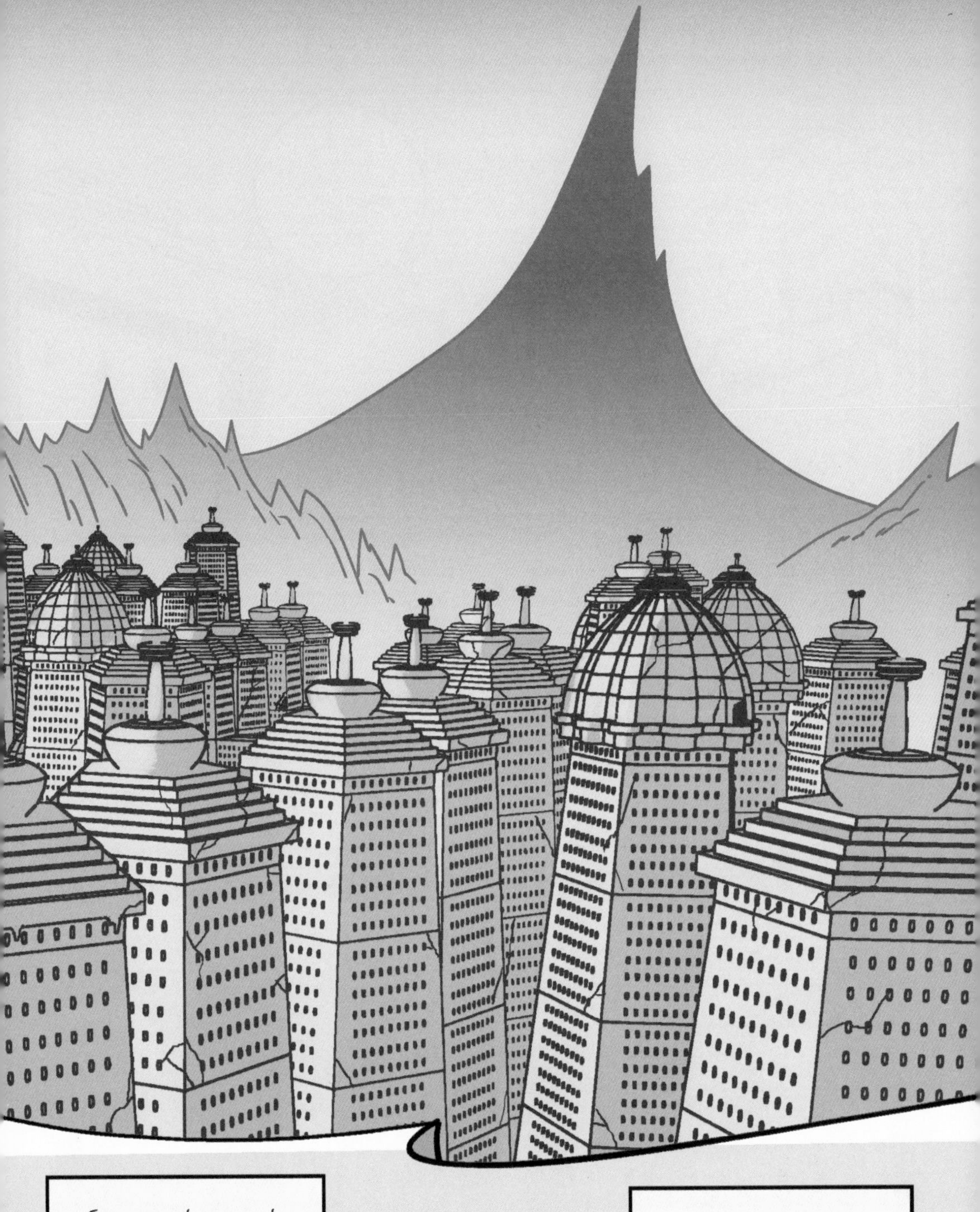
For a second we gasped in admiration of the scene's unearthly cosmic beauty – and then vague horror began to creep into our souls...
For this far violet line, pinnacled against the western sky, could be nothing but the dreaded Kadath in the Cold Waste.

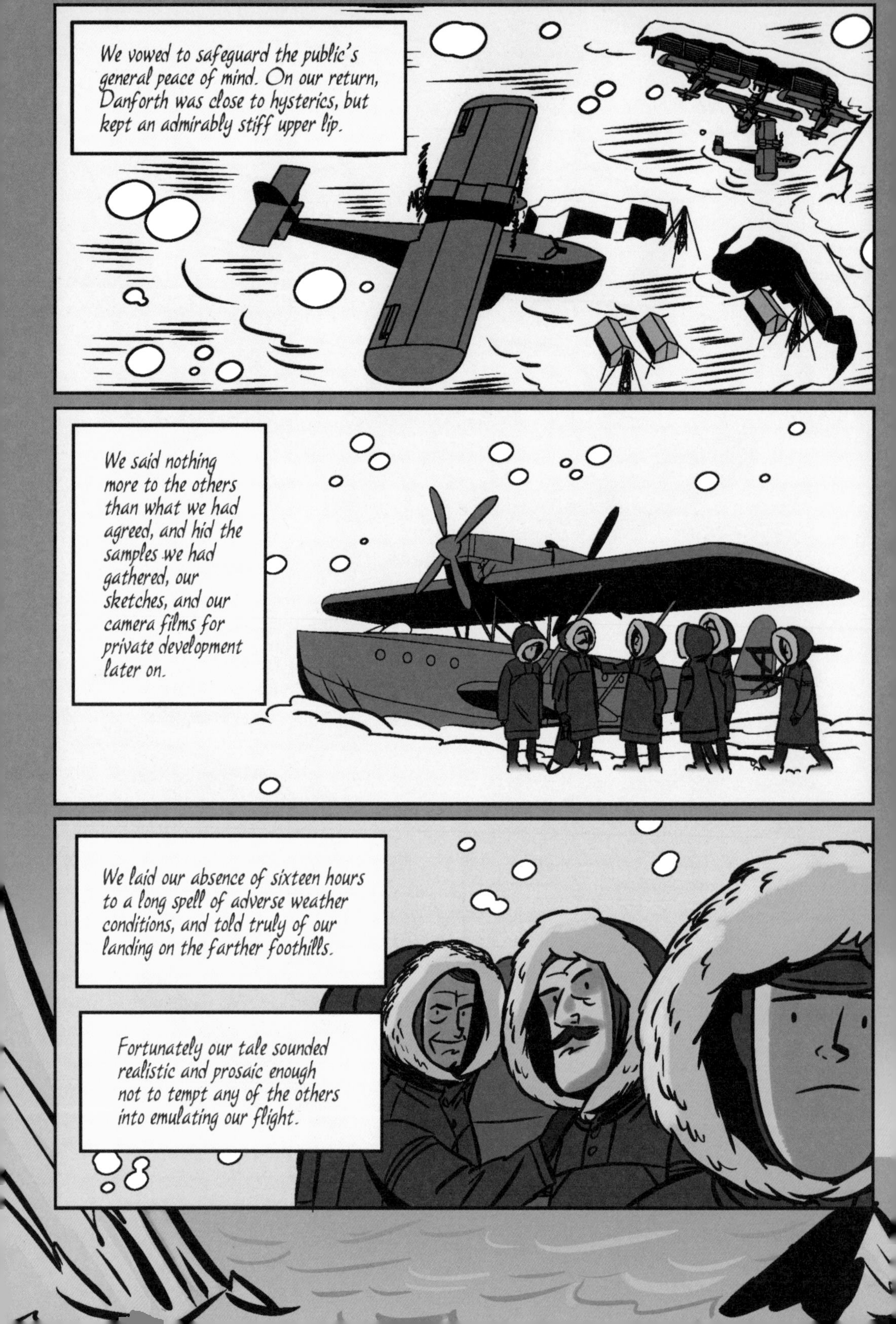
We vowed to safeguard the public's general peace of mind. On our return, Danforth was close to hysterics, but kept an admirably stiff upper lip.
We said nothing more to the others than what we had agreed, and hid the samples we had gathered, our sketches, and our camera films for private development later on.
We laid our absence of sixteen hours to a long spell of adverse weather conditions, and told truly of our landing on the farther foothills.
Fortunately our tale sounded realistic and prosaic enough not to tempt any of the others into emulating our flight.

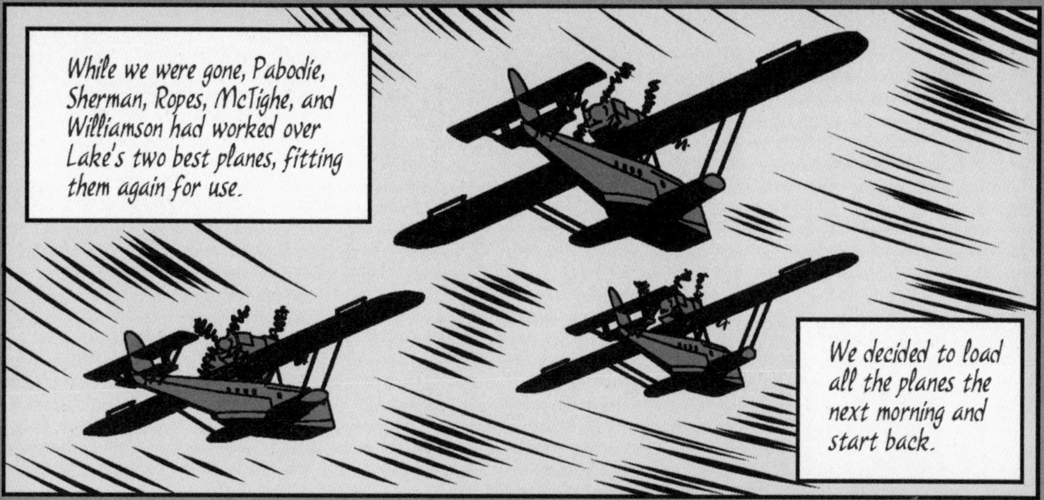
While we were gone, Pabodie, Sherman, Ropes, McTighe, and Williamson had worked over Lake's two best planes, fitting them again for use.
We decided to load all the planes the next morning and start back.

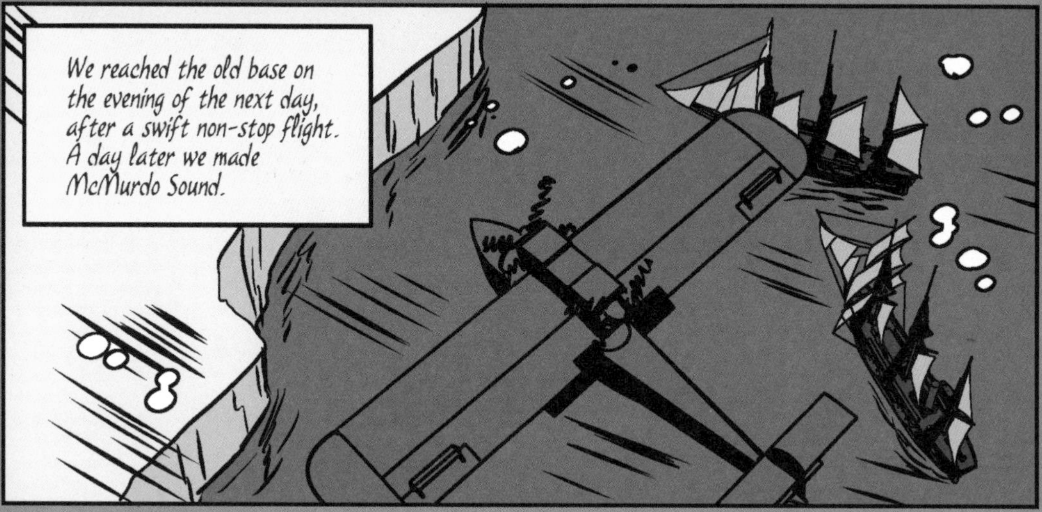
We reached the old base on the evening of the next day, after a swift non-stop flight. A day later we made McMurdo Sound.

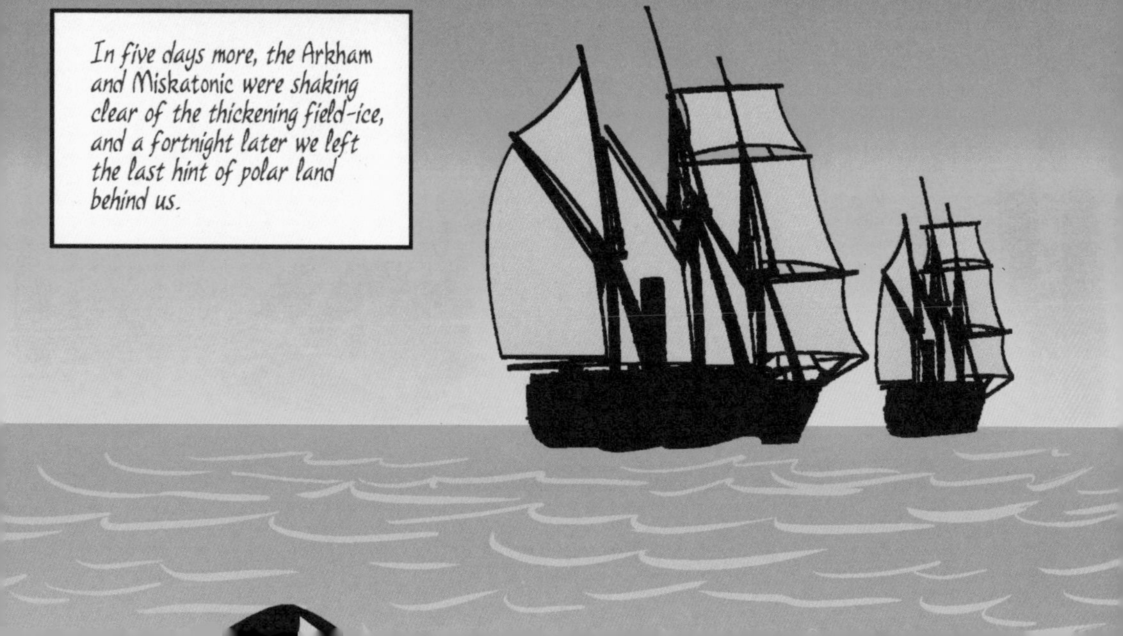
In five days more, the Arkham and Miskatonic were shaking clear of the thickening field-ice, and a fortnight later we left the last hint of polar land behind us.

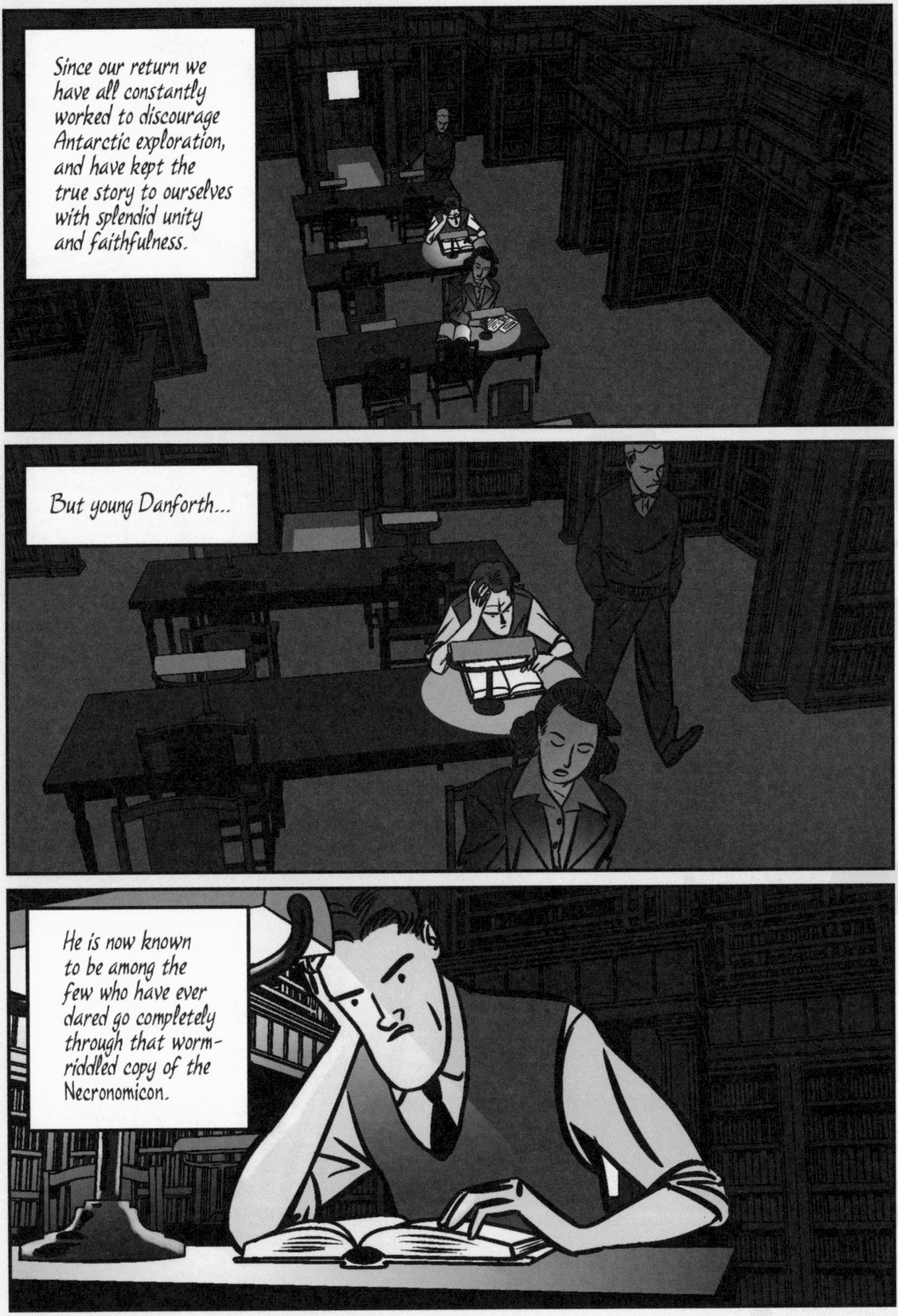
Since our return we have all constantly worked to discourage Antarctic exploration, and have kept the true story to ourselves with splendid unity and faithfulness.
But young Danforth...
He is now known to be among the few who have ever dared go completely through that worm-riddled copy of the Necronomicon.

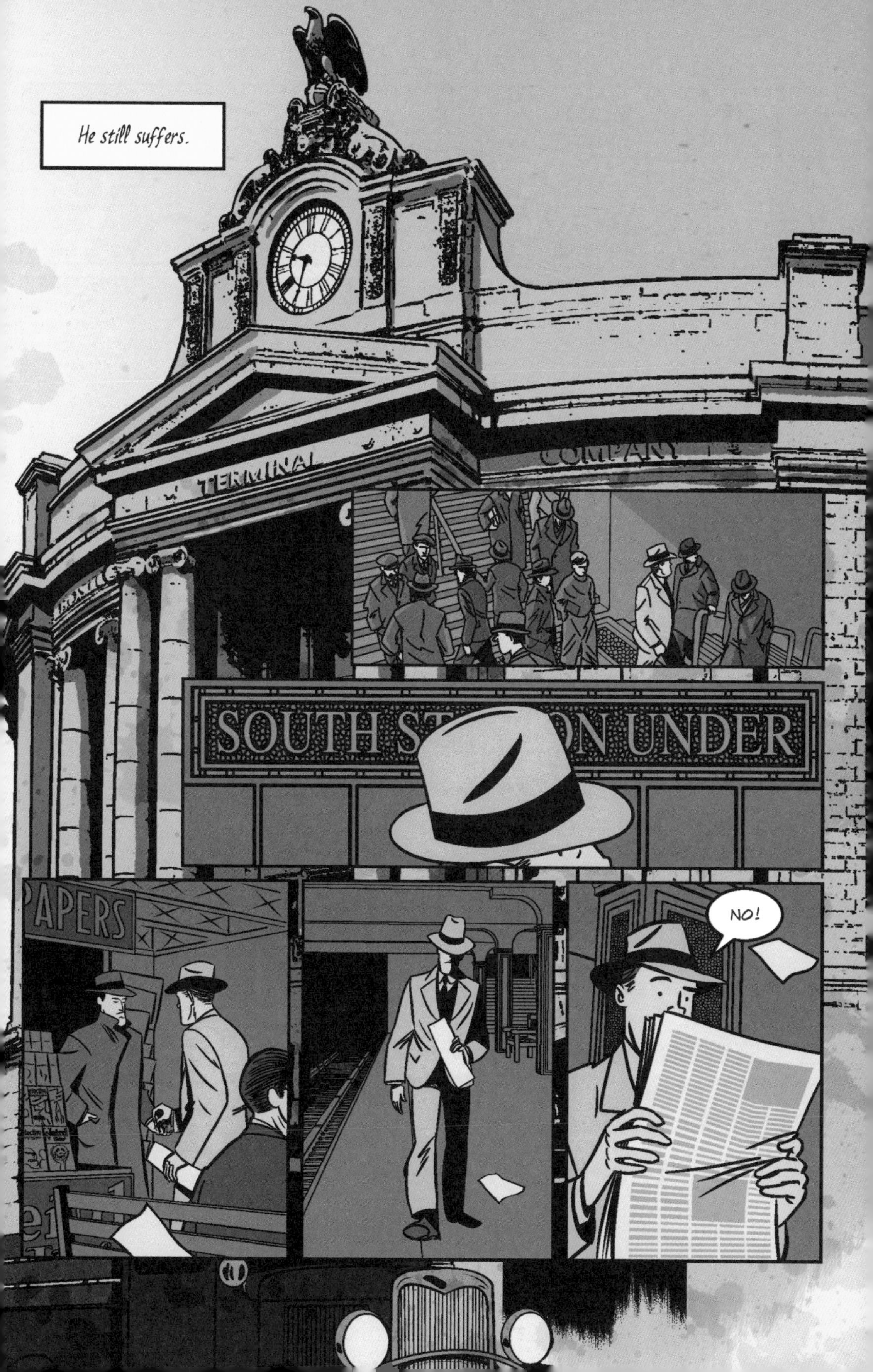
He still suffers.
TERMINAL
COMPANY
SOUTH ST ON UNDER
PAPERS
NO!

OTHER TITLES
ILLUSTRATED BY I.N.J. CULBARD

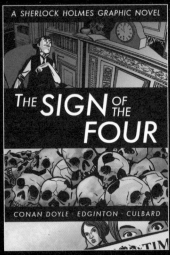

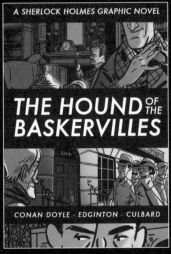

THE SIGN OF THE FOUR
978-1-906838-04-1 £14.99

A STUDY IN SCARLET
978-1-906838-01-0 £14.99

THE HOUND OF THE BASKERVILLES
978-1-906838-00-3 £14.99

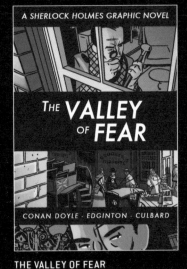

THE VALLEY OF FEAR
978-1-906838-05-8 £14.99

THE PICTURE OF DORIAN GRAY
978-0-9558169-3-2 £12.99